Practical
SpellCraft

A First Course in Magic

Leanna Greenaway

HAMPTON ROADS

I would like to dedicate this book to Mamma Witch,
who for many years has been my inspiration and my salvation.
May you continue to wave your wand.

Cover design by Jim Warner
Cover illustration © Jennifer Hewitson

Hampton Roads Publishing Company, Inc.
Charlottesville, VA 22906
Distributed by Red Wheel/Weiser, LLC
www.redwheelweiser.com
Sign up for our newsletter and special offers by going to
www.redwheelweiser.com/newsletter/.

ISBN: 978-1-57174-754-9

Library of Congress Cataloging-in-Publication Data
Names: Greenaway, Leanna, author.
Title: Practical spellcraft : a first course in magic / Leanna Greenaway.
Description: Charlottesville : Hampton Roads Pub., 2017. | Originally   published: New
York : Sterling Pub. Co., c2003. | Includes bibliographical   references.
Identifiers: LCCN 2016044538 | ISBN 9781571747549 (5.5 x 8.5 tp : alk. paper)
Subjects: LCSH: Witchcraft. | Charms. | Magic.
Classification: LCC BF1566 .G724 2017 | DDC 133.4/3--dc23
LC record available at https://lccn.loc.gov/2016044538

Printed in the United States of America
M&G
10 9 8 7 6 5 4 3 2 1

Contents

1

Observations

For centuries, people have considered that spellcasting has something disturbing or sinister attached or to it. When one considers fairy tales that date back over the years, the witch is observed as a wart-ridden old woman, wearing a crooked black hat, with a cat or familiar by her side and a big bubbling cauldron before her. It is only now, in the 21st century, that society is starting to see that witchcraft was (and still is) just another religion or way of life. The Harry Potter mania has opened up many people's minds to Wicca, and, although some still consider it a sinful practice, many are keen to explore this interesting, gratifying, and rewarding faith.

It is not easy to give an accurate date for the origins of Paganism, but it is certainly known to be pre-Christian. It is amusing to consider, when we come up against the sceptics of society, that each and every one of us has practiced witchcraft or Pagan rituals at some time in our lives. Shocked? Well it's true. We have all been introduced to superstition at some stage of our lives, and many of the "old wives' tales" from years gone by emanated from the ancient Pagans. The following are a number of well-known examples.

Present-Day Rituals That Have Pagan Roots

THE BIRTHDAY PARTY

The child can expect a gathering of people at his birthday party, a cake, and a number of colored candles, and he is encouraged to make a wish while blowing out the candles. This is one of the oldest known Pagan traditions and is said in many modern manuals to be the first form of candle magic that a child practices. Later in this book, we will cover the subject of candle rituals at length.

THE WEDDING

The traditional wedding ceremony is another ancient Pagan or Wiccan custom. In a Pagan ceremony—or as it is more commonly known, a "Handfasting"—the bride and groom initially tie the knot for only a year and a day. The expression "to tie the knot" comes from the ritual that is performed by the couple, during which they would tie and knot a rope around their hands, symbolically binding the two lovers. The period that the couple spends together settles whether or not they are compatible. If, after the year and a day, they remain in love, they then go on to hold another ceremony, this time making a permanent commitment to each other. This custom has become the engagement or betrothal that precedes a wedding.

THE CEREMONY

A High Priest or a High Priestess performed the ceremony, usually outdoors or in a specified place of worship, such as a church. Three hundred years ago, Pagans and Christians had no option but to share their churches, so it was widely acceptable for Pagans to marry in church.

THE RINGS

Gold rings were exchanged during a wedding, and these symbolized the goddess, the wheel of the year, and the circle of life. The ring was then placed on the third finger of the left hand because it was believed that a vein ran directly from this finger to the heart. The wearing of the rings was a sign to everyone that the couple was bound together by the unity of Handfasting. This has carried over into modern practice in Christian weddings and, as we know, in the Christian faith the couple exchange rings while they make their vows.

THE ALTAR AND THE CANDLES

Most Christian churches conduct the majority of their ceremonies at the altar. In the Pagan faith, two candles (usually white) were placed on the altar and represented the male and the female. As the candles burnt down, the spirit of the flame was said to represent the spirit of the couple, and this traveled upward in the direction of the universe to be accepted by the goddess herself.

For centuries, Christians have worshiped their God by reciting prayers over a lighted candle at weddings, baptisms, and so forth, but the Pagans also deliver their invocations over candles while worshipping their gods and goddesses.

THE RICE AND THE CAKE

Once the wedding ceremony is complete, it is customary to throw rice or confetti over the happy couple. In Pagan and Wiccan weddings, the idea was to tap into the spirit of the fertile grain or seeds so that the couple could absorb it, thus ensuring that they would have a good and prosperous harvest and never starve. In ancient times, biscuits were crumbled over the heads of the couple to ensure the bride's fertility. It must have been somewhat irritating for the bride on her wedding day, having groomed herself to a high standard, then to be showered with handfuls of crumbled biscuits!

Thankfully, however, throughout the course of time, this ancient tradition has changed. In days gone by, it was fashionable for the bride and groom to slice a fruitcake, both holding the knife together and showing their love by kissing over the top of it. This was supposed to guarantee that together they would bear many children. By sharing the cake with their guests, they were indirectly sharing the magical energy of their love and passing it on to everyone present.

THE GARTER

A buckled leather garter was a mark of the witch bride's rank. The number of buckles on the garter represented the number of covens that had originated from the witch bride's, and this established her status in society. These garters were often handed down within families, passing from mother to daughter to granddaughter. This tradition has been lost over time, and now very few people actually know the true meaning of the garter; it has become just a slightly saucy part of the wedding outfit.

When we research and study a Pagan faith, it becomes clear that many similarities are shared between the Christians and the Pagans. It saddens those who believe in Pagan traditions to realize that, even after all these years, witchcraft is still considered to be a taboo subject. Religion has contributed to numerous wars throughout history.

We must try to remember that a religion or way of life has to be personal to the individual. No one has the right to insist that any person should follow a faith that is not true to them. I am a great believer in the old saying, "If it feels right, then believe it. If it doesn't, then don't!" We are all aware that every religion carries good and bad issues. Some folk profess to be Christian while going out of their way to hinder or damage others. Some Pagans curse or cause the destruction of others.

There are good and bad people the world over. Prejudice comes from refusing to give an individual the freedom to express him- or herself in the way he or she would wish, and also by refusing to research or understand a faith before assuming the worst. I hasten to add that the majority of Wiccans are peace-loving people who perform rituals only for the good of others. They believe in the healing powers of nature, and they worship our planet with great passion. So let us allow every man to follow his true path and hinder no one!

2

How I Became a Witch

Many people ask me how I became a witch, and I have come to the conclusion that a witch isn't something you become or decide to be; rather, it is something that is deep-seated and inbred from an early age. When I was a child, some kind of inner knowledge triggered me to follow the path of Wicca. Indeed, I started to meditate from about six years of age. Although my mother was a white witch herself, I was far too young to understand, and she hadn't even started to teach me the Wiccan ways at that time, because she herself was waiting for me to follow my chosen path in life.

Being the sort of person she is, when I asked if I could attend Sunday school, she happily arranged for me to go. I'm sure that if I had decided to become a minister of the church, she would have supported me in any way she could. At this young age, no one pushed me into joining the Pagan faith; I just instinctively knew it was a part of me.

As I got older and reached my teenage years, I asked my mother many questions. She answered them honestly, always adding that just because she believed in the Wiccan practices, it didn't mean I had to follow suit. She always tried to leave me with an open mind, preferring not to influence me. I became intrigued when I saw her perform Tarot readings for others—although she kept her spellcasting private. It wasn't long before I figured out that the things she was doing in her everyday life were just what I wanted to do in mine!

Soon thereafter, I gave my dear mother the nickname "Mamma Witch," and much to her annoyance, the name has stuck to this day. Although she raises an eyebrow at me every now and then, she accepts the title gracefully, and I have even received the odd birthday card signed "Mamma Witch."

As a young person, I was superstitious and ritualistic. I truly believed that if I said things over and over again, they would eventually come true—and occasionally they did! Again, this was something that had never been introduced to me. Only now, after years of researching more into the Pagan ways, have I realized that I had been performing rituals for the best part of my life without having been shown how.

Mamma came from a family that believed in magic. Her grandmother and great grandmother were practicing clairvoyants, so she inherited their gifts and wisdom, which she passed on to me. I was around thirteen when Mamma began to share her secrets with me, and I would report back to her after my regular practice sessions of meditation. She then started to teach me a few very simple spells. Being a typical teenager, I found this frustrating, because I wanted to jump across the planet, climb the highest mountain, and plunge into casting the most powerful spells known without taking the time needed for the preliminaries. Oh, I had a lot to learn—and in this book, you will read about some of my mishaps.

However, it is only when I look back that I see how much I owe to my poor mamma, quietly going about her faith without any problem, who suddenly found herself faced with a young, sprightly, up and coming little witch who was urgently demanding her knowledge and "borrowing" her spell books!

Do You Have the Potential?

If you have an inclination toward witchcraft in this lifetime, it is probable that you were a witch in a past life. I have taught spellcraft for many years, and occasionally one of my students will tell me that they don't feel as though they are learning something that is really new to them, but they are simply being reminded of things that they already knew. In some cases, students were unconsciously using some of the techniques in their daily life, and this came up in the exercises that they were given as part of their course work.

If you are reading this book, it is likely that you have used witchcraft in a previous life. Witchcraft is within us, it is part of us, and if it prompts us to let it out, we should follow our hearts.

3

Some Background—and Foreground

S ome call Wicca a religion, but as such, it is an unusual one, and there are many opinions as to the origin of the words "Wicca" and "witch." Some historians say that the word "Wicca" is a contraction of the Old Saxon word "Witega," which meant a prophet or sorcerer. It has also been taken to mean "wise person," in the sense of someone who knew how to use plants as medicines for humans and for animals in the days before the development of modern medicine and veterinary practices.

It is said that witchcraft and Wicca developed out of the ancient Druidic mother goddess religion. Wicca doesn't have rules and regulations of the kind that we associate with standard religions, but there are practices that over a period of time have become traditional. Basically, Wicca is personal to many of those who follow it. In every country, there are solitary witches who use individual practices but also many who learn and develop their skills with help from fellow witches.

One common belief is encapsulated in the following Wiccan *rede* (saying): it was apparently first stated by Doreen Valiente in 1964, as the couplet: "Eight words the Wiccan Rede fulfill / An [if] it harm none, do what ye will."

The word "witchcraft" is most likely derived from the practice of the old English Wicca craft, meaning "the way of the wise" or "wise-craft." The word "Wicca" also has a modern meaning derived from the words candle and candlewick. From the beginning, witches have always worshipped nature and placed great importance on their surroundings. Witches are environmentally friendly, due to the fact that they strive to preserve our planet, and they also take great care not to harm others. Witches believe in the "god" and the "goddess" being the true life forces. They consider "Mother Nature" to be paramount.

Paganism covers a broad range of religions, generally polytheistic. In plain English, this means a belief in more than one god. I have also seen Paganism described as including a pantheistic religion, meaning one in which trees, mountains, rivers, and other natural phenomena are considered to be sacred.

Neither witchcraft nor Paganism have anything to do with devil worship, but despite this, there are people who believe that all Pagans and witches practice such things. The Christians may have believed that the devil exists, but whether this is true or not, the devil is not linked to Paganism—so why does society insist on continuing to believe this myth? Although witchcraft is becoming more acceptable throughout the world, this nonexistent connection to the devil still leaves some people feeling uncomfortable.

During the time of the persecutions, it was known that the Pagans worshipped the goat. This belief was part of their faith. Pan, the Horned God, was nothing more than an icon of reverence. When Christians set out to convert others to their religion, they denounced every practicing Pagan as a devil worshipper, turning their much-respected Horned God into the devil. Contrary to belief, few witches practice witchcraft for the purposes of greed or to work on a lower vibration. The majority of witches have only the good of others in mind, and they work hard to create a sense of balance and well-being among their fellow men.

The public antipathy toward witchcraft means that witches, who regularly worship their gods, do so in a solitary fashion. Many people these days actually take an interest in these old traditions without even realizing it, just as they also look into such things as homeopathy, acupuncture, and reflexology. For instance, the green issue has meant that many of us are starting to worry about our planet, and we are becoming aware that soon it may be too late to save it. Most people read a horoscope in newspapers and magazines, and this has encouraged an interest in the Tarot and the nature of the earth's energies.

At some point in life, many people have been intrigued by the word "witchcraft." While some have the thirst for this knowledge, others fear it because they are not yet ready to open their minds or to understand its true meaning. If you are inclined toward a Pagan lifestyle, sooner or later you will encounter people who consider you are dabbling with hocus-pocus or some form of evil, but this naïve notion is wrong. If you are interested in Paganism, it is probably best not to mention this to those who don't understand. Paganism may be one of the oldest religions on earth, but it is now growing in popularity once again.

Few people broadcast the fact that they are witches, but witches can be found practicing their rituals everywhere and in every town and country of the world. Due to the unfortunate stigma attached to Wicca, many of them practice their craft covertly. Some even keep their beliefs from members of their families, so as to prevent ignorance and prejudice from casting a black cloud over their relationships.

Witches in ancient times relied wholly on the fruits of the land to survive. Therefore, they would study moon patterns and seasons, worshipping the fertility of the soil and thanking Mother Nature with prayer. These people were totally in tune with their earth; they only killed animals for food, and they grew their own vegetables, using the properties in plants for medicines and oils. They believed that the preservation of the earth was of the greatest importance. Many studied the skies regularly to know when to plant their crops. These individuals were decent and hard working, and they lived in harmony with their neighbors. They worked in communities and went about their business without conflict or struggle.

At one time, the Pagans outnumbered Christians; they lived side by side in their surroundings and tolerated the others' religion. They may have even shared their churches, many having different entrances and separate altars. The Pagan altar was said to face either the west or the north, the Christians followed the Jewish tradition of facing toward Jerusalem.

As time passed, Christians began to outnumber others, and they wanted to reign supreme, but to their consternation, the Pagans believed devoutly in their faith, and they resisted conversion. The Christians, at various times, believed that there was no room for any other religion than their own, so they began a reign of terror. For this reason, many Pagans did convert out of fear that a fanatic would kill them and harm their families.

Over the centuries, the Christians discredited the Pagan beliefs, and they termed Wicca or witchcraft an evil principle. Those Pagans and witches who would not convert to Christianity began to practice their religion in secret, often taking to secluded countryside locations, such as moors or forests, to worship their gods. They thrived in their secret assemblies and worshipped mainly in groups, which became known as covens. Some of these Pagan groups were hunted down and murdered. The Christians then continued to spread the notion of devil worship throughout the world, and many ordinary folk, who respected life's elements and worshipped the seasons, were persecuted and murdered.

The 17th century was the worst period of persecution in both England and America; most everyone is familiar with the famous witch hunts and witch trials of Salem, Massachusetts. Witch hunt hysteria scooped up people who practiced pagan beliefs as well as many people who were innocent of practicing any form of witchcraft. The estimated number of deaths around the world during this period of persecution is said to run between three and four million.

Modern Witches

To have faith is to believe in what you cannot yet see and what others cannot perceive, your reward is to see what you believe.

Contrary to belief, not all witches are female, and there are many male witches. There are male and female witches in every town and village in the world. I am proud to be a witch, yet even I hasten to add that there are a few members of my family who do not know of my beliefs. Only when they feel ready to open their minds and understand me will I choose to tell them.

The witches of today are much the same as they were hundreds of years ago. Obviously, times have changed, but most of us have a passion for the supernatural, because we believe that there is more than what we see and do in our daily lives. We think more deeply about situations that others simply dismiss. We believe that nothing in this life is a coincidence and that everything is down to fate and destiny, and when we look back on our lives, we can see that the difficult or disappointing times we have endured have contributed to our present wisdom. We recognize that this planet resembles a big classroom and that we reincarnate many times in order to learn; so when we pass our exams in one subject, we move on to the next.

If you look back on your life and take the most challenging situation you found yourself in, you will find that you came out the other side as a stronger person and that some good has come out of your time of trouble. Life is composed of dilemmas, and fate will place obstacles in our way. If you don't have any problems yourself, you may feel drawn to help or influence others whose lives are more complicated.

We start each lifetime carrying a suitcase full of knowledge that we have brought with us from our previous lives—although it is sometimes hard for us to understand how these energies affect us. For example, you may have known what it's like to starve in a previous life, and this might make you a food freak in this life. You may have had eleven children in a previous existence, so in this lifetime you become aware of what it is like to be infertile. These are hard lessons, but when we pass over from this life into the spirit world, all of our questions will be answered.

It is said that you have to experience every human emotion possible to evolve spiritually and to gain the wisdom you need to progress up the spiritual ladder. For example, an adult who has been abused as a child would be a better counselor than one who had not suffered in this way. If you have really strong views on a subject, such as child abuse, or if you suffer from a horror of drowning, it may be that you have experienced this in a previous life. The theory is that you have to be familiar with a situation to be able to empathize.

Have you ever sat quietly in a chair and wondered why on earth you are here? Have you questioned such things as being sick, working too hard, struggling for money, or simply being alive? Witches believe in reincarnation. Think deeply for a moment and ask yourself whether it would be a waste of time to come to the planet just the once. What would be the point to it all? Why go through all the emotions we have to experience during a lifetime just to end up as nothing?

Many of you may have looked at a child and felt that he has been here before or that he is an old soul—and many are. I always felt so much older and wiser than my alcoholic grandmother. Even though she was forty years older, in the spiritual sense it was obvious that she was a young soul!

There is an old saying: "You cannot teach what you haven't learned." Through modern witchcraft, you can learn how to exercise control over your life and to understand the importance of the "life force" and the significance of your fate. This book will help you unravel the mystery and symbolism that exists, as you learn how to tune in to it. It is really just like learning a new language, and once you get the hang of it, there will be no stopping you. So come on this journey with me and allow me to help you find your higher consciousness.

Wiccan Beliefs

Witches worship the earth around us. We seek to live in harmony with nature and to do no intentional injustice to any creature or person in our path.

- The moon is important to witches. We believe that it affects the energies surrounding the planet and controls the situations and the moods of mankind.

- We feel we are able to attune with powers that the untrained person cannot. We understand the supernatural, and we look deeper into issues for solutions to problems.

- We believe in both an outer world and an inner world, which we call our spirit world.

- We believe that the earth is a place of learning. We come here for a short time and learn life's lessons to further our spiritual development, then we return to our home—the place from which we initially came, the spirit world. We may choose to come back to earth for another lifetime to overcome problems and try to achieve grace.

∾ To a certain extent, we eschew authoritarianism, because we believe that we are all equal, but we appreciate and respect that there must be certain people who set out laws and rules for our own well-being.

∾ We do not believe in Satan or the devil as defined by the Christian tradition. We understand that there are evil influences in this life, but we consider the word "devil" a Christian concept that has been used to frighten people throughout the centuries.

∾ We do not advocate ill will toward another being nor do we delight in power or influence over others. We work only for the good and well-being of other individuals. These are some of the beliefs that many witches and Pagans regard as their basic ground rules.

∾ Take a moment to consider what induced you to become interested in magic. Look back to when you were small. Did you have some underlying knowledge or understanding? I think you will find that you did.

4

The Sabbats and Halloween

All religions celebrate certain holidays and festivals, and Pagans have their own, which are called sabbats. Rather than falling on specific dates each year, the sabbats are based on the position of the sun, so they vary from one location to another.

The Sabbats

The following is a basic list that fits the scene in the US and Northern Europe. However, these dates will need to be switched around for witches who operate in the southern hemisphere, or moved to some extent in regions that are farther north or south in relation to the equator.

WINTER SOLSTICE—YULE (ON OR AROUND DECEMBER 22)

Long before Christianity, the winter solstice was associated with the birth of the "Divine King." The sun is known to represent the male divinity in most Pagan traditions, so this festival is famous for the "return of the sun god" when he is reborn of the goddess.

IMBOLC (FEBRUARY 2)

This Sabbat marks the revival of the goddess after giving birth to the god. During this time, the god is just a child, whose daily development is strengthened throughout the lengthening of the days. With Imbolc, we see the beginning of spring, when early flowers start to bloom, and the trees and plants germinate.

SPRING EQUINOX—OSTARA (ON OR AROUND MARCH 21)

As the young god matures and develops, Ostara welcomes the first valid day of spring, when the days and nights are equal in length, and we begin to see new growth with buds and shoots present on the trees. Needless to say, this sabbat links with Easter, but it was also the start of the new year in the ancient Roman calendar.

BELTANE (APRIL 20–MAY 1)

The goddess herself symbolizes the earth, and as the soil and surroundings ripen, the young god conveys his love to her. This is the time to revel in the first flowers of summer, and they are gathered as a tribute during this celebration.

SUMMER SOLSTICE—MIDSUMMER (ON OR AROUND JUNE 21)

The longest day is known as the time when the first harvest of herbs shares its reward with us. This is also the traditional time for Handfasting and wedding ceremonies.

IUGHNASADH (AUGUST 1)

The animals are nearly fully grown as we celebrate our first harvest. Plants are setting their seeds in readiness for the coming cycle. Autumn approaches, and the sun (also son) still glows intensely in the sky.

AUTUMN EQUINOX—MABON
(ON OR AROUND SEPTEMBER 21)

The days and nights are equal once again, and the second harvest continues. Gardens should be in full bloom, and a slight chill in the air warns us of the colder months to follow.

SAMHAIN (OCTOBER 31–NOVEMBER 1)

This brings us to the final harvest. The earth says a sad farewell to the god, but we are also aware that he will be reborn again by the goddess. We reflect upon the past year and practice divinatory acts. This is a time to remember and communicate with those who have died and passed into spirit.

HALLOWEEN

Many of us celebrated Halloween (Samhain by its more familiar name) when we were young, and our children still do so. This holiday is also known as All Hallows Eve, and it is followed by All Souls Day. However, how many of us know its true significance?

In Celtic Ireland in the 5th century BC, the local Celtic folk were known for being particularly close to the earth and its vibration. They celebrated the end of the summer on October 31 and November 1, seeing this as the start of their year and thus their

New Year's Day. This marked the beginning of the winter that lay ahead, so to their thinking, this was a time that was closely linked to death. They believed that on this day, the spirits of those who had died would return to earth and connect with the living. People would welcome closely related spirits, but make an effort to ward off evil ones, which they did by making their homes cold and bleak and by wearing ghoulish costumes.

They believed that this was a particularly powerful time during which to predict future events, either on a personal level or connected to crops, harvests, and the general life of their community. They were surviving in an unpredictable world, so these foresights were an important part of their lives. Such predictions could warn them of coming danger or give them comfort and a feeling of security as the hazardous winter approached.

As a symbolic event, the Druids would build large, sacred bonfires, and they sacrificed crops and animals to their Celtic deities. Druid shamans dressed in animal skins and animal heads, while they proceeded to give predictions to those who were present.

The trick-or-treat tradition has various origins, but it seems to stem from the idea of offerings. The Druids believed that certain spirits would cause chaos and destruction if they were not pacified at this time of the year. Everybody in the village or locality needed to be involved in this activity, sacrificing a small amount of their own stock of food. Some people visited the Druids with offerings, while in other cases, peasant folk went from door to door, collecting bread, cheese, eggs, and so on, to take to the Druid priests in preparation for the religious ritual.

Apples were considered to be sacred to the goddess. At this time of the year, the people played games with apples, and they even used them for divination. The best-known game is apple bobbing, in which a number of apples are placed in a tub or half-barrel of water, whereupon they float to the top. Single people who were hoping to marry would have their hands tied behind their backs, and then they would try to catch an apple between their teeth. The first person to catch and bite an apple would marry during the coming year.

By the 8th century, Christianity had influenced most of the Celtic lands, so it was during that time that Pope Boniface IV renamed November 1 "All Saints Day" to honor the saints and martyrs. It seemed that the pope was following the tradition of replacing ancient festivals with Christian ones, a form of what we now call "politically correct."

Most of the old Celtic traditions drifted away during the course of time, but something of the ancient Halloween tradition has hung on into modern times. Children still dress up in costumes that represent witches and ghosts, while adults dress up and go to fancy-dress Halloween parties. Next time you hand out sweets to children, go to a riotous Halloween party, or play "bob for an apple" with your children on October 31, remember its ancient significance and spare a thought for its past meaning—and also for those loved ones whom you have lost.

5

Tools and Concepts

Now I will introduce you to the tools that you will need to perform spells. None of these are costly or difficult to make or to obtain, and you should enjoy putting these together. Let us start with the five-pointed star that is known as the pentagram. The word "pentagram" is made up of *penta,* which comes from the Latin for the number five, and *gram,* which in this context means something that is written or drawn.

Many of you will be familiar with the symbol of the pentagram or five-pointed star. In magic, this represents protection; it also symbolizes the five elements of earth, air, fire, water, and spirit. This is sometimes also referred to as the "endless knot."

The pentagram dates back to around 3500 BC, and it has been associated with myth and magic in various countries of the world. Since ancient times, it was known to protect its owner, and it was frequently worn as an amulet to celebrate a happy homecoming. Should the pentagram be turned upside down, the image then becomes the Pagan god Pan, otherwise known as the Horned God. Christians equated the pentagram to the devil, and sadly, among some people, it has lost its true meaning, becoming a symbol of evil and devil worship.

It is quite common for someone to see a pentagram when entering a witch's house. Many witches and spellcasters own pentagrams made from glass or cloth with the symbol embedded in some way. Some may wear the five-pointed star around their necks as jewelry, and it is quite usual to recognize a witch by this much-loved symbol. It is absolutely essential to have a pentagram before you start to cast spells, as this affords protection.

How to Make a Pentagram

You need to consider making a pentagram about the size of a small dinner plate, and it should have a flat surface, because you will need to be able to put candles on it. Making a pentagram need not be costly, as there are many materials that you can use when making it.

Here is a suggestion that involves using thick card. Take a dinner plate; trace around it and then cut out the circle shape. After this, you should draw the pentagram symbol, ensuring that each point of the star touches the edge of the circle. Once you have done this, you can leave it as it is or decorate your pentagram in any way you wish, perhaps by painting colored symbols or flowers on it. The design is unimportant, but customizing it to suit your own taste makes it individual to you. From now on, this pentagram will be your source of defense and protection. Later on, you may decide to collect pentagrams or to make a selection of them to work with.

Another inexpensive way to create a more elaborate pentagram is to ask a glass cutter to cut you a glass circle about four-
teen inches in diameter. You can then buy some "peel-and-stick"
lead to complete the pentagram. You might consider download-
ing a picture of a pentagram from the Internet and blowing it up.
You can then stick this to the glass. Don't use such downloads for
commercial purposes, though, because they are invariably under
copyright restrictions. Once you have your pentagram, it is important that it is always placed or hung with the single point at the
top. Only those who engage in the dark side use the pentagram
upside down.

CHARGING YOUR PENTAGRAM

Once you have completed making your pentagram, it is essential
to charge it. This is a simple procedure, but it is necessary for the
purpose of spellcasting.

Find a quiet room that is free from hustle and bustle and sit
very still, holding your pentagram in front of you. At this stage,
you must close your eyes and try to clear your mind. Spend about
five minutes doing this. Imagine that you have an invisible eye in
the center of your forehead (this is known as the inner, or third,
eye). Now picture a bright purple light radiating from your inner
eye and pointing directly at the pentagram. Concentrate on this
for a few minutes. The next step is to summon the archangels of
the universe to bring love and protection by reciting the following
invocation:

I conjure thee, archangels of the cosmos,

To aid me in my magical workings.

I ask for your influence and protection,

From the evil that this earth breeds.

Send forth your power and light

To this symbol before me.

Let it bring protection into my home

And all that surrounds me.

So mote it be.

You will need to recite these words with meaning and concentration if the invocation is to work. After this, put the pentagram on the ground and sit quietly for a few more minutes with the palm of your hands facing down on the pentagram, still imagining the purple light radiating from your inner eye. Your pentagram is now charged, and you can safely put it away until you have completed the next stage.

During this experience, you may feel the palms of your hands becoming very hot, and some people also experience a feeling of light-headedness. This kind of thing is quite normal and is nothing that should alarm you; it is simply that this kind of exercise opens up your subconscious and focuses your power and strength toward the pentagram. Those of you who have never done anything like this before may find it a relaxing but strange experience.

The Altar

The altar and the things that are placed upon it create a geographic focus or special place for performing magical rituals. Some witches don't feel the need for an altar, but I am a firm believer that it is best to have a base to work from.

When you begin to create your altar, the procedure is similar to that of creating the pentagram in that you need to make it special to you. Every witch designs his or her altar in a different way, because there is no definite right or wrong way to do this. Some Wiccan teachings indicate that the contents of the altar should be laid out in a certain manner and that specific tools must be placed in a certain way. In my view, you need to feel at one with your place of work, so you must create it according to your own taste and requirements.

Place the altar in a quiet room where you can work without being disturbed. Don't worry about the direction that your altar faces, because any directional spells included in this book can be done without the altar. As long as you are comfortable with your arrangement, that is what matters. Like the pentagram, your altar is absolutely personal to you.

Not everybody has a home that is spacious enough to house a full sized altar, and some witches don't wish to broadcast that they cast spells. I prefer to have my altar on display at all times, as I find this convenient. I regard it as a piece of furniture, as my partner took great care when making it for me, and I feel that it enhances my room—but I fully appreciate that I may be in a minority. Some witches take the alternative option of a portable altar that they can bring out whenever they need it. This usually consists of a cloth that can be laid on the floor. This is also handy for those who travel around and need to take their altar with them.

Your first task is to choose a table or surface to use as a base. This can be a large table, a coffee table, or indeed a card table, because size is not important. Next, you will need to find an altar cloth, and this can be as simple or as elaborate as you like, as long as it covers the surface of your table. I have a stunning purple cloth that I bought at a street market, and my mother (who is a good needle woman) embroidered a wonderful silver pentagram in the center for me. Once you have found your cloth, lay it on the table and place your charged pentagram in the center. You will find, as I did, that you experience a sense of pleasure when you start to see your creations coming together in this way.

All good witches keep a large supply of candles at hand, because they play such a huge part in the cleansing factor. The next step is to buy or acquire three or four tall, white tapered candles and some attractive candlesticks. How you position them on the altar is not important. Some books recommend that these should be placed to the north, south, east, and west, but your spells will work however you situate them, so move them around until you find the optimum position.

Salt and water are important items for your altar, as these will give you the highest form of protection and purity during your work. I suggest that you place two small bowls, one of salt and the other filled with water, somewhere near your pentagram. It is important to spellcasting to include items that symbolize the five elements; you can add a small bowl of earth and arrange the three bowls in a pleasing pattern.

Initiated witches tend to have a more varied altar that includes a variety of tools, but the ones that I have mentioned are the basics. Incense enhances spells, although it is not absolutely necessary to burn this during invocations. Your personal altar can have anything you like placed on it. It is usual for any altar to include something to represent the four elements of earth, air, fire, and water, while the element of "spirit" will be summoned during spellcasting to assist you in your magical tasks. The fire will be in the flame of the candles once they are lit.

I feel a great affinity toward crystals, as they seem to have a magic of their own, so I keep at least three on my altar at all times. I am also an avid believer in the power of animals, and I actually went through a stage in my life when everybody who knew me would buy me a symbol of an eagle for Christmas or for my birthday. This was either a piece of jewelry or an ornament. I couldn't understand why this was, as I had never been particularly fond of eagles. Fairies, unicorns, and mermaids, yes—but not eagles.

My mamma wisely pointed out to me that the eagle represents power and strength, and it may be that the eagle was my own personal power animal or totem. I sat on this thought for some time, until I accepted it as the case. You may be drawn to a particular animal or feel an affinity with a certain creature. If this is so, then try to obtain a picture or symbol of it and place it on your altar along with the rest of your finds, as it may well add to your power and increase your magic.

So in summary, you will need at least the following basic items for your altar:

- ❧ a table

- ❧ a cloth or piece of material to cover the table—color is not important, but white and purple are highly recommended, as these are known to be spiritual colors

- ❧ a charged pentagram placed directly in the center of the altar

- ❧ four tapered white candles

- ❧ small bowls of salt, water, and earth

- ❧ optional: crystals, pictures, or any other possession that you feel drawn to

Always keep matches or a cigarette lighter nearby for lighting the candles. Later in the book, you will be shown how to perform spells using five candles, so this might be a good time to shop around for five identical candle holders. From my past experience, I advise you to buy ones that are completely heat proof, such as brass or copper, because otherwise your spells might be more explosive than you would wish them to be.

Music is always calming and restful when performing rituals, so look around for some meditative music to inspire you. Meditation is used with candle magic, and music provides the right kind of ambience.

Finally, please do bear in mind that candles are a fire hazard. Small children will try to blow out a candle during spellcasting—and with candle magic, that is not a good idea! My advice is to keep candles, matches, etc., locked away, and preferably work when small children are asleep or elsewhere.

The Book of Shadows

Some of you might be familiar with the "Book of Shadows." Every practicing witch has one of these books, which she consults on a daily basis. The Book of Shadows is a notebook in which you record your spells and any other psychic or unusual experiences that you may have. It is books such as these that give the basis for the countless ancient spells that are practiced today, and some of these have been handed down through generations of families. Old books have been shared with other witches in the past, and this has helped to keep information on spells, candle rituals, and effigies alive through the ages.

The contents of each Book of Shadows vary from one witch to the next, due to the intensely personal nature of this book. Any Book of Shadows will contain a diary of the year's moon patterns. These can be written or attached in some way. As the Book of Shadows tends to remain with the witch for a lifetime, many prefer to keep the information on moon phases separate, because these will need to be updated every year.

The Book of Shadows also includes basic information on candle rituals—the influence that is attached to the colors and symbols that relate to candle magic. Some witches prefer to keep a record of their own spells and to record the results in the Book of Shadows. This kind of record will help a witch to adapt a spell that doesn't work as proficiently as it should. The main thing to bear in mind is that this book is private, and only the owner should ever read it.

I remember when I was younger, desperately wanting to sneak a peek at Mamma's book. Whenever she consulted it, I would hover around and try to look over her shoulder to see the contents. It was only when I became a little more mature that she allowed me to view it, and to my amazement, it was virtually the same as my own book, with its descriptions of premonitions, meditations, and dream analyses. The Book of Shadows also works as a dream diary.

WRITING YOUR OWN SPELLS

Spells may be old or new, traditional or modern, but many are born in the hearts and minds of witches. I followed books (such as this one) for many years before I developed the confidence to create my own rituals, but now I write nearly all of my spells myself. Spells can be more effective when you compile them yourself, because you focus all your attention on the task at hand.

When you begin to write your own spells, note them down in your Book of Shadows. Make sure that you follow the influences of the colors and moon phases. If a spell doesn't work the first time around, don't give up; adjust it and try again. You will need to be realistic with your requests, and you need to ensure that you perform the spell because it is needed, rather than doing it just to see what happens.

Start with something simple. For instance, if you are short of money, sit down quietly, and try to write a short poem that asks for your financial needs to be met. When you are happy with what you have written, light a candle, and recite it. Say it every day until improvement comes. If you like, create an amulet or talisman for your purpose, and place this on the altar while you are reciting your spell.

Dreams and Astral Travel

Many witches believe that "spirit" can send messages through dreams, so it is important to jot them down immediately upon awakening, because we can quickly forget them. I tend to remember my dreams regularly, and while many dreams are insignificant, there are times when I know that I have had an important dream, as it is particularly vivid or it carries a message. Keep your book by your bedside; if you wake up and remember a dream, write it down so that you can interpret it when you have time to think about it.

There are many different types of dream sleep. It is said that when we sleep, our spirit enters a different vibration. Even today, scientists cannot fully explain the purpose of dreams. Some theories state that our subconscious minds wind down after the day by rejuvenating our mental energies. I am certain that this is correct to some extent, but spiritual people believe that our souls are able to leave our bodies while still attached by an invisible umbilical cord, and that they can take astral journeys. Because witches were so regularly connected to the idea of traveling the astral, the more ancient concept was that the witch would fly on a broomstick.

Those who are spiritually inclined have recorded their dreams over the years; it is said that if we need them, our spiritual guides come to us when we are sleeping, traveling the astral plane. Have you ever dreamed of flying? Many of us have, but have you ever looked at it from another point of view? In the Wiccan faith, to dream of flying is said to represent the spirit leaving the earthly body to travel to places that we could never reach while awake. Record what you learn in your dreams in your Book of Shadows.

6

The Moon and Magic

The moon has always been seen as having a magical influence. Our ancestors worshipped it, but they were unaware of the scientific and spiritual reasons for its influence on their world. With the onset of technology, scientists are becoming more aware of the moon's influence, and it is interesting to note that many who look into lunar matters find themselves getting in touch with their spiritual nature.

Those who have traveled in space find themselves taking a deeper look into their spiritual and religious beliefs, so it would appear that these intensely practical people begin to search for answers based on a far more spiritual level than a scientific one.

The moon is approximately 241,250 miles away from earth, and it takes about twenty-seven days to complete an orbit around the earth. The earth orbits the sun, so the combined movement of the moon around the earth and the earth's orbit means that it takes around twenty-eight days to reach the same position in the succeeding zodiac sign.

The mystical moon has been worshipped in many religions, and as people began to link its influence to us on the earth, they also began to understand its connection to ourselves. The moon is traditionally linked to womankind and to the functions that are connected to the right side of the brain, which is associated with creativity and insight. Men also possess these attributes, but they are usually more highly developed in women.

There are a variety of theories about the effect of the moon on our minds and bodies, some of which have been proven and others that are pretty fanciful. However, it is known that certain "lunatics" become overexcited or violent during a full moon phase. Several years ago, I studied the behavior of a six-year-old boy who had several conditions linked to autism, and I discovered that he was far less stable and settled around the time of the full moon; indeed, his behavior became uncontrollable then. Once the phase passed, he appeared to be more receptive to other people and also happier in himself. After six months of close observation, I discovered that this cycle occurred every month.

As far back as the earliest time, the sun, moon, and stars have been linked to women and pregnancy. When we start to look for female connections to the moon, we see that the female menstrual cycle takes roughly 29.5 days to complete, which is just over one lunar month, or the period between two full moons. Pregnancy is around 280 days long, which is the approximate number of days between ten full moons and one half moon. It is uncanny how fertile women are affected by the lunar cycle.

We know that the moon has influence over the tides and also over the behavior of mollusks and other sea-born animals, so it is not surprising that it has such an influence over men and women.

Some argue that this is a coincidence, but I don't believe in coincidences, and I know that our world and the surrounding planets still keep many of their secrets.

You may wish to note down your own moods during the course of each month, and see if they link with the phases of the moon. You may be surprised at the results. I know that I feel more spiritual around the time of the full moon. I cannot explain why this is, but I know that I tend to meditate more, and I have the urge to perform visualization techniques at that time. Around the dark of the moon, I sometimes find myself in awkward situations in which I am unaccountably faced with obstacles and problems.

Some people feel calmer during a new moon phase, and others are happier during a full moon phase. Astrologers tell us that some of this depends upon where the moon was when a person was born, but whatever the reason, it really is worth keeping an eye on your own feelings and recording your findings in your Book of Shadows. This may even be able to help you to avoid certain situations and to take more control of your life.

The Phases of the Moon

It is so important to remember the significance of the moon when you begin to cast spells. Never conduct a ritual without consulting your calendar first, and always be aware of what the moon is doing. There are some rituals that can be performed at any time, but some state specifically that the moon should be in a certain phase for you to obtain the desired result. If you cast a spell at the wrong lunar phase, it is unlikely to work properly, and it may only give half the result that you wanted.

When I look into the sky and see the moon in all its glory, I definitely feel that there is more to this existence than purely functioning on a daily basis. You have only to see the magic that it portrays, the way it makes its presence felt, and the comfort that many of us feel from its light to understand this feeling.

If the sky is clear and the moon is in view, try sitting outside for a half hour or so and staring at it. Many people have experienced wonderful sensations while doing this, and some of the best clairvoyants have predicted many an occurrence after doing this. Science tells us that the moon has a tremendous effect on our planet—so why not also upon us?

Throughout time, witches have conducted rituals out of doors under the moon, and they consider that spells conducted in this way hold more importance. I believe this. I have done the occasional ritual outside—although not "sky-clad," I might add! I usually whisper the incantation, because I don't want my neighbors to think that I am totally crazy, but I do feel at one with the earth at such times, and I come away afterward with a sense of well-being.

(NOTE: If you are into astrology, you will know what is meant by suggesting that it may be worth avoiding magical work when the moon is "void." This means the times when it is toward the end of a sign of the zodiac and cannot make any aspect to any other planet before it changes to the next sign.)

THE FULL MOON

Research shows that when the moon is full, there are more traffic accidents, murders, and suicides than at any other time during the lunar cycle. The term "lunatic" comes from the idea that those who are unfortunate enough to endure mental problems have more than the usual number of difficulties during the full moon phase. It is also well known that criminals are more active during this phase and that accident and emergency departments of hospitals are busier.

The full moon period is known to endow greater power when one is conducting rituals. In olden times, witches performed spells for love during this phase, and this leaves us wondering whether people may feel more romantic when the moon is full. One thing is certain: when rituals are done correctly, the moon really works its magic during this phase.

THE WAXING MOON

When the moon is waxing (growing larger), witches cast spells that are designed to improve situations. These spells are useful if your life is standing still. The energies at this time seem to work in a very positive fashion, and if rituals are performed correctly, they usually bring about the desired results very quickly.

One has to understand, though, that some conditions are not meant to change right away. You can try to make things advance, but they will not do so if fate wishes you to stand still and look at a red traffic light. In this case, you have no recourse other than to wait until the spirit world feels that your personal traffic light is ready to turn green.

THE WANING MOON

When the moon is waning, it is growing smaller. We all find ourselves in trouble at some time or another, and we can all be faced with situations that are out of control. The waning moon is a brilliant time in which to push away the black cloud that sometimes hangs over us and to push away any negativity or bad influences.

Sometimes we may feel as though we don't have the strength to tackle certain individuals or the confidence to face up to our fears. By spellcasting during this phase, we can draw toward us the power that allows us to take control, to strengthen our inner selves, and to become more assertive. We know that it is our fate to find ourselves in certain predicaments, but when this happens, it is up to us to work our way out of them rather than allow them to swamp us.

THE NEW MOON

Of all the lunar phases, most witches find this the most positive for bringing about new situations. Many changes occur around the time of the new moon, including relationships, career events, births, and house moves. If you really need a change, perform a ritual at this time, and you should soon start to see your life transforming.

THE DARK OF THE MOON

This phase begins three days before a new moon and clears once the new moon appears. It is not the nicest of phases to live through. Only a very experienced witch can take a chance on casting a spell at this time, and unless it is absolutely vital, you should avoid doing so.

This is because many of those who work on the dark side tend to perform their rituals during a dark moon phase. It is not known how many of these individuals practice what we know as black magic, but even if just two or three hundred people were to be casting spells in a harmful fashion at the same time, a negative energy would be picked up by the more sensitive among us.

If you study the moon patterns, you will discover that your life becomes muddled and jumbled at the dark of the moon. When recording your mood changes in your Book of Shadows, jot down the situations that you are faced with at this time. If you ignore this advice or don't check the moon's phase calendar before performing a spell, the ritual is likely to be affected by destructive energies that will either cause it to work improperly or even to produce unpleasant consequences. Experienced witches will perform rituals that eliminate negativity around this moon phase before getting down to anything, but I would strongly suggest that you simply avoid doing any magical work during the dark moon phase.

Lunar Dates

For those of you who haven't the time or the inclination to watch the sky, here is a "lunar ephemeris" (moon diary) that will take you up to the end of the year 2027, and which you can photocopy and put into your Book of Shadows. Remember that a waxing moon is one that is moving from new to full, and a waning moon is one that is moving from full to old. The former occurs halfway between the new and full moon, the latter halfway between the full and new moon.

2017	Moon
12 Jan 2017	Full
28 Jan 2017	New
11 Feb 2017	Full
26 Feb 2017	New
12 Mar 2017	Full
28 Mar 2017	New
11 Apr 2017	Full
26 Apr 2017	New
10 May 2017	Full
25 May 2017	New
9 Jun 2017	Full
24 Jun 2017	New
9 Jul 2017	Full
23 Jul 2017	New
7 Aug 2017	Full
21 Aug 2017	New
6 Sep 2017	Full
20 Sep 2017	New
5 Oct 2017	Full
19 Oct 2017	New
4 Nov 2017	Full
18 Nov 2017	New
3 Dec 2017	Full
18 Dec 2017	New

2018	Moon
2 Jan 2018	Full
17 Jan 2018	New
31 Jan 2018	Full
15 Feb 2018	New
2 Mar 2018	Full
17 Mar 2018	New
31 Mar 2018	Full
16 Apr 2018	New
30 Apr 2018	Full
15 May 2018	New
29 May 2018	Full
13 Jun 2018	New
28 Jun 2018	Full
13 Jul 2018	New
27 Jul 2018	Full
11 Aug 2018	New
26 Aug 2018	Full
9 Sep 2018	New
25 Sep 2018	Full
9 Oct 2018	New
24 Oct 2018	Full
7 Nov 2018	New
23 Nov 2018	Full
7 Dec 2018	New
22 Dec 2018	Full

2019	Moon		2020	Moon
6 Jan 2019	New		10 Jan 2020	Full
21 Jan 2019	Full		24 Jan 2020	New
4 Feb 2019	New		9 Feb 2020	Full
19 Feb 2019	Full		23 Feb 2020	New
6 Mar 2019	New		9 Mar 2020	Full
21 Mar 2019	Full		24 Mar 2020	New
5 Apr 2019	New		8 Apr 2020	Full
19 Apr 2019	Full		23 Apr 2020	New
4 May 2019	New		7 May 2020	Full
18 May 2019	Full		22 May 2020	New
3 Jun 2019	New		5 Jun 2020	Full
17 Jun 2019	Full		21 Jun 2020	New
2 Jul 2019	New		5 Jul 2020	Full
16 Jul 2019	Full		20 Jul 2020	New
1 Aug 2019	New		3 Aug 2020	Full
15 Aug 2019	Full		19 Aug 2020	New
30 Aug 2019	New		2 Sep 2020	Full
14 Sep 2019	Full		17 Sep 2020	New
28 Sep 2019	New		1 Oct 2020	Full
13 Oct 2019	Full		16 Oct 2020	New
28 Oct 2019	New		31 Oct 2020	Full
12 Nov 2019	Full		15 Nov 2020	New
26 Nov 2019	New		30 Nov 2020	Full
12 Dec 2019	Full		14 Dec 2020	New
26 Dec 2019	New		30 Dec 2020	Full

2021	Moon
13 Jan 2021	New
28 Jan 2021	Full
11 Feb 2021	New
27 Feb 2021	Full
13 Mar 2021	New
28 Mar 2021	Full
12 Apr 2021	New
27 Apr 2021	Full
11 May 2021	New
26 May 2021	Full
10 Jun 2021	New
24 Jun 2021	Full
10 Jul 2021	New
24 Jul 2021	Full
8 Aug 2021	New
22 Aug 2021	Full
7 Sep 2021	New
20 Sep 2021	Full
6 Oct 2021	New
20 Oct 2021	Full
4 Nov 2021	New
19 Nov 2021	Full
4 Dec 2021	New
19 Dec 2021	Full

2022	Moon
2 Jan 2022	New
17 Jan 2022	Full
1 Feb 2022	New
16 Feb 2022	Full
2 Mar 2022	New
18 Mar 2022	Full
1 Apr 2022	New
16 Apr 2022	Full
30 Apr 2022	New
16 May 2022	Full
30 May 2022	New
14 Jun 2022	Full
29 Jun 2022	New
13 Jul 2022	Full
28 Jul 2022	New
12 Aug 2022	Full
27 Aug 2022	New
10 Sep 2022	Full
25 Sep 2022	New
9 Oct 2022	Full
25 Oct 2022	New
8 Nov 2022	Full
23 Nov 2022	New
8 Dec 2022	Full
23 Dec 2022	New

2023	Moon	2024	Moon
6 Jan 2023	Full	11 Jan 2024	New
21 Jan 2023	New	25 Jan 2024	Full
5 Feb 2023	Full	9 Feb 2024	New
20 Feb 2023	New	24 Feb 2024	Full
7 Mar 2023	Full	10 Mar 2024	New
21 Mar 2023	New	25 Mar 2024	Full
6 Apr 2023	Full	8 Apr 2024	New
20 Apr 2023	New	23 Apr 2024	Full
5 May 2023	Full	8 May 2024	New
19 May 2023	New	23 May 2024	Full
4 Jun 2023	Full	6 Jun 2024	New
18 Jun 2023	New	22 Jun 2024	Full
3 Jul 2023	Full	5 Jul 2024	New
17 Jul 2023	New	21 Jul 2024	Full
1 Aug 2023	Full	4 Aug 2024	New
16 Aug 2023	New	19 Aug 2024	Full
31 Aug 2023	Full	3 Sep 2024	New
15 Sep 2023	New	18 Sep 2024	Full
29 Sep 2023	Full	2 Oct 2024	New
14 Oct 2023	New	17 Oct 2024	Full
28 Oct 2023	Full	1 Nov 2024	New
13 Nov 2023	New	15 Nov 2024	Full
27 Nov 2023	Full	1 Dec 2024	New
12 Dec 2023	New	15 Dec 2024	Full
27 Dec 2023	Full	30 Dec 2024	New

2025	Moon	2026	Moon
13 Jan 2025	Full	3 Jan 2026	Full
29 Jan 2025	New	18 Jan 2026	New
12 Feb 2025	Full	1 Feb 2026	Full
28 Feb 2025	New	17 Feb 2026	New
14 Mar 2025	Full	3 Mar 2026	Full
29 Mar 2025	New	18 Mar 2026	New
13 Apr 2025	Full	1 Apr 2026	Full
27 Apr 2025	New	17 Apr 2026	New
12 May 2025	Full	1 May 2026	Full
27 May 2025	New	16 May 2026	New
11 Jun 2025	Full	31 May 2026	Full
25 Jun 2025	New	14 Jun 2026	New
10 Jul 2025	Full	29 Jun 2026	Full
24 Jul 2025	New	14 Jul 2026	New
9 Aug 2025	Full	29 Jul 2026	Full
23 Aug 2025	New	12 Aug 2026	New
7 Sep 2025	Full	27 Aug 2026	Full
21 Sep 2025	New	10 Sep 2026	New
7 Oct 2025	Full	26 Sep 2026	Full
21 Oct 2025	New	10 Oct 2026	New
5 Nov 2025	Full	25 Oct 2026	Full
20 Nov 2025	New	9 Nov 2026	New
4 Dec 2025	Full	24 Nov 2026	Full
20 Dec 2025	New	8 Dec 2026	New
		23 Dec 2026	Full

2027	MOON
7 JAN 2027	NEW
22 JAN 2027	FULL
6 FEB 2027	NEW
20 FEB 2027	FULL
8 MAR 2027	NEW
22 MAR 2027	FULL
6 APR 2027	NEW
20 APR 2027	FULL
6 MAY 2027	NEW
20 MAY 2027	FULL
4 JUN 2027	NEW
18 JUN 2027	FULL

3 JUL 2027	NEW
18 JUL 2027	FULL
2 AUG 2027	NEW
17 AUG 2027	FULL
31 AUG 2027	NEW
15 SEP 2027	FULL
29 SEP 2027	NEW
15 OCT 2027	FULL
29 OCT 2027	NEW
13 NOV 2027	FULL
27 NOV 2027	NEW
13 DEC 2027	FULL
27 DEC 2027	NEW

Some months contain two new or full moons. Such occasions are called blue moons, which is where the old saying "once in a blue moon" comes from. There is nothing special about these as far as spells and magic are concerned, but a month containing two new moons might be particularly lucky.

7

The Right Time

Hourly Planetary Ephemeris

Here is something else that you can photocopy and put into your Book of Shadows, as you may wish to use this information when performing certain very special spells. Some of the spells in this book mention the fact that they work best if they are performed on a particular day of the week, but if you want even more planetary energy for an especially important spell, you may wish to choose the right hour for your spellcasting. The chart that follows will show you which planet rules each hour of the day. I have added some helpful information about the energies of each of the planets at the end of this chapter, and this will help you to understand why certain days and times tune in to particular types of spells. Even when using spells that don't mention any specific time or day, you can choose to enhance their effects yourself by selecting a helpful hour or day.

THE HOURLY EPHEMERIS

Hour	Sun	Mon	Tue	Wed	Thu	Fri	Sat
a.m.							
1	Sun	Moon	Mars	Mercury	Jupiter	Venus	Saturn
2	Venus	Saturn	Sun	Moon	Mars	Mercury	Jupiter
3	Mercury	Jupiter	Venus	Saturn	Sun	Moon	Mars
4	Moon	Mars	Mercury	Jupiter	Venus	Saturn	Sun
5	Saturn	Sun	Moon	Mars	Mercury	Jupiter	Venus
6	Jupiter	Venus	Saturn	Sun	Moon	Mars	Mercury
7	Mars	Mercury	Jupiter	Venus	Saturn	Sun	Moon
8	Sun	Moon	Mars	Mercury	Jupiter	Venus	Saturn
9	Venus	Saturn	Sun	Moon	Mars	Mercury	Jupiter
10	Mercury	Jupiter	Venus	Saturn	Sun	Moon	Mars
11	Moon	Mars	Mercury	Jupiter	Venus	Saturn	Sun
12	Saturn	Sun	Moon	Mars	Mercury	Jupiter	Venus
p.m.							
13	Jupiter	Venus	Saturn	Sun	Moon	Mars	Mercury
14	Mars	Mercury	Jupiter	Venus	Saturn	Sun	Moon
15	Sun	Moon	Mars	Mercury	Jupiter	Venus	Saturn
16	Venus	Saturn	Sun	Moon	Mars	Mercury	Jupiter
17	Mercury	Jupiter	Venus	Saturn	Sun	Moon	Mars
18	Moon	Mars	Mercury	Jupiter	Venus	Saturn	Sun
19	Saturn	Sun	Moon	Mars	Mercury	Jupiter	Venus
20	Jupiter	Venus	Saturn	Sun	Moon	Mars	Mercury
21	Mars	Mercury	Jupiter	Venus	Saturn	Sun	Moon
22	Sun	Moon	Mars	Mercury	Jupiter	Venus	Saturn
23	Venus	Saturn	Sun	Moon	Mars	Mercury	Jupiter
24	Mercury	Jupiter	Venus	Saturn	Sun	Moon	Mars

(Note: When Daylight Saving Time is in operation, deduct one hour; e.g,, 7 p.m. becomes 6 p.m.)

THE SUN

Perform spells for celebrations, leisure events, holidays, games, sports, and hobbies. This is a good time for spells concerning love affairs and for anything to do with children. If you want to succeed in an exam or an endeavor or to become famous, choose a sun hour.

THE MOON

This is a good hour for spells that will improve your psychic powers and also spells for home, household, and family matters, especially those connected to mother figures.

MARS

Tackle anything that requires action and activity during a Mars hour. This is a good hour for spells that help you to stand up for yourself and to fight for justice. Mars rules sex, passion, and lovemaking, so choose a Mars hour and a Tuesday for these spells.

MERCURY

Mercury rules communication of all kinds, so whether you want to get a message through to someone, improve your ability to communicate, or change your vehicle or otherwise improve your mode of transport, choose this hour.

Sporting activities and anything relating to younger people will be aided by spellcasting on this hour. Mercury is especially associated with health, so spells that are designed to improve your own health or to make someone else feel better should be performed at this hour.

JUPITER

Jupiter is associated with long-distance travel, so this is a great day or hour in which to make travel spells or to ask Jupiter to bless a journey for you. Any business dealings that involve overseas customers or foreigners will be successful if performed on this hour.

This is the best hour for anything concerning legal matters and important documents. This planet rules education, religion, philosophy, and spirituality. It is also associated with gambling—especially gambling on horse racing.

VENUS

Venus was the Roman goddess of love, so if you are planning a romantic meeting with a lover or even with a potential mate, choose a Venus day or hour for your spell. Venus is also associated with personal finances and the goods that you own or that you wish to own, so spells for these things would be successful if performed at this time.

SATURN

Saturn will help you to develop wisdom and enlist the help of older people, father figures, or those who are in positions of authority over you. This is the hour to use if you wish to enhance your status, to achieve success in business, and to be taken seriously by others.

8

Good Vibrations

One of the first rules when casting spells is to clear your mind and free yourself of negativity. If you cannot focus intensely on your ritual, it is unlikely to work. This is all about believing in what you are doing, because if you conduct a ritual with half your mind on what you're going to cook for dinner that evening, you can't expect to get any results.

When you throw yourself into something heart and soul, it is more likely to succeed—and it's exactly the same with magic. Believe in what you are doing, and be adamant in your mind that it will work. Once you have seen for yourself how incredible spells can be, it will become second nature for you to believe in them.

Throughout the centuries, "white" magic has been known to be extremely powerful, but we have to remember that "black" magic is just as dominant. Without even realizing it, you could cast a spell and unwittingly find yourself delving into the dark side, but don't let this put you off, because you will soon learn how to be in complete charge of your spell. You may have heard the term "positive thought"; well, every practicing Pagan works hard to clear his or her mind, not just when performing magic but in everyday life.

A Thought Is a Living Thing

Imagine this situation. You enter a room, and two or three people are laughing uncontrollably. You don't know what they are laughing about, and they can't tell you because they are laughing so hard that they can't speak, but you automatically begin to giggle or chuckle. In exactly the same way, if you walked into a room and saw someone crying her heart out, you would feel upset and concerned. Emotions are contagious. Every single thought or feeling that you send out will be picked up, even when you are not physically close to the sender.

It is common for people who are very closely connected to feel one another's emotions when they are apart. This is a well-known phenomenon with twins and siblings, but can also extend to friends and acquaintances. Some say that telepathy plays an important part in these sensations. Most of this thought transference is harmless, but witches use rituals to enhance the power of the mind and to fortify their spells. In addition, just as we can use our influence to improve and bring about good things for people, so we can (sometimes even without meaning it) send out what used to be referred to as the "evil eye."

The first rule is to be positive. Never perform a spell with the intention of injuring or harming anyone or with selfish intent, as this is neither the Wiccan way nor the behavior of a true witch. Don't try to gain power or control over others; don't try to change them, except by using love and causing no detriment to them. We have to guard against overstepping the mark. This has nothing to do with the devil or summoning evil spirits, but it has everything to do with the power of the mind and directing our energies in a positive fashion.

Cause and Effect

Have you ever heard the saying, "What you sow, so shall you reap"? This is a Pagan saying, although some also call it the law of karma. I am a devout believer in the Pagan theory that says, "What you send out, you eventually get back." If you send out love and light, you attract the same thing back threefold, warding off negative influences in the process. Should you send out hate, ill will, or malice, sooner or later it will do a U-turn and come tumbling back, reinforced.

This is why it is essential that, when conducting a ritual, you always perform it with the best of intentions. Remember the old Wiccan saying, "Harm none." Just take into account the importance of mind power. Keep your spells full of light, and the magic will work in a positive way. Start taking revenge or influencing situations for your own greed, and you're likely to fall flat on your face.

Protection against Black Magic

Very few of us will be unlucky enough to come across a person who works on the dark side. Many think that it is nonsense and that magic cannot be used to harm anybody. This notion is untrue.

Black magic is very much alive and practiced by many occultists working on the dark side throughout the world. Just as many of us want to create a positive influence with our spells, others can summon a darker vibration, causing unwanted negativity for those they seek to harm.

When I was working as a clairvoyant in the north of England, a lady client of mine became involved with a man who later professed to be a Satanist, or "devil worshipper." He called himself a black witch. This is absolutely ludicrous, because black witches don't exist, and Pagans don't believe in the devil! After discovering this, the lady ended the relationship, but the man took the breakup badly.

Over the next six months, he monitored her lifestyle, convincing her that every problem she faced and every mishap she and members of her family were enduring were down to his magic. It was true that her life had taken a downhill slide. She had lost her job and crashed her car. While her son was touring Australia, he contracted a mystery illness that no doctor or consultant could fathom.

She came to me in terror, believing that the man was behind her run of ill luck. It did seem to be a little more than coincidental, so I took her theory on board and proceeded to guide and advise her as to the best way to banish him.

This kind of scenario is a matter of one person seeking to control another, and it is comparable to the bully-versus-victim scenario. A bully feeds on the other person's fear, and it gives him a sense of power and supremacy. We all know that if we stand up to the bully, the oppressor loses his control and gives up. I gave my client this advice and told her that if she continued to show him she was weak, he would inevitably feed on her fear and use it to his own advantage.

I'm sure she found it difficult to be confident in this situation, but she changed her approach completely and tackled this "black lord" head on. The next time he contacted her, she listened to his threats and then mentioned that she had consulted a real white witch who had given her a spell to perform that would counteract any evil that he sent her. She also advised him of the rebound effect and told him that every black thought he sent her way would return to him threefold.

This guy was not easy to scare, and he set out to find the white witch who was working against him. I kept candles burning day and night for a while! After three weeks of intense protection spells, news came that the man had lost an enormous amount of money and had had to give up a five-bedroom house; he finally left the area in pursuit of a new life.

I doubt that many people will ever come across such a hateful character as this. However, we all cause jealousy or make enemies at some point, and if they send hateful thoughts to us, we will receive their negative influences. It is always wise to protect ourselves from psychic attack—and however strong or forceful the other person appears to be, we must maintain confidence in ourselves. I have included a few spells for protection for you to use if you think someone is directing negative thoughts at you.

Love Spells

One grey area is that of love spells. Many of my clients have asked me to perform love spells for them. This may sound harmless, but

if these are not done properly, they can bring disastrous consequences. Having made this point, I will give you some spells for
love later in the book.

Now that you have some basic ground rules in place, we can
start to look at the art of spellcasting more clearly.

9

Candle Magic

There are many forms of spellcasting that give successful results, but candle rituals are effective and easy to manage. This works as a form of prayer that is recited over a lighted candle. Many religions use candles in association with prayer, so this method is well understood and nothing out of the ordinary. Before you cast a spell with candles, it is important to understand exactly what is happening.

Candle rituals are a form of magic that is based on what witches refer to as the "elemental." This means that we summon the five elements of earth, air, fire, water, and spirit. We also call upon the angels of the planets so that we invoke all the energies on a universal level. Each planet has an angel as its ruler, and these angelic forces can be called upon to assist in candle magic.

It is imperative, when using candle magic, to follow the rules with precision. Each angel represents a specific day and each has its own color. Always use the correct candle color for the specified day. Each planet, angel, and color has its own influence, so you need to use the right color candle on the right day for your spell to be successful.

Blessing and Cleansing the Candle

It is imperative when performing a spell that your candle is cleansed. Candles are very quick to pick up on vibrations, so if the person who makes or packs the candle or prepares it for sale is holding any negative energy, it will be incorporated into the candle.

Having said that, candles seem to have a kind of intrinsic goodness. In the same way that a child from a bad family may struggle to become a good adult, so candles that suffer bad beginnings will struggle to give good results. It is important to cleanse the candle to obtain the benefit and effectiveness of its power.

Always use a new candle; never use one that has been lit before. Place a bowl of spring water on your altar and wet your hand. Wipe your wet hand over the candle while reciting the following blessing:

I bless this candle in preparation for my work,

I rid it of any negative properties,

Making it pure in every way.

So mote it be.

This must be done every time you use a candle for spellcasting. If you are using more than one candle for a spell, bless them all.

Inscribing Your Candle

Inscribing a candle gives it more potency, so always try to make the message as clear as you can when inscribing it. You can write as much as you like on the candle, as long as you ensure that your wish is readable and precise. Using a sharp knife or a pin, inscribe the name of the person for whom you are performing the spell.

For instance, if you wish to perform a love spell for yourself, inscribe your own name on the candle and the words, "To attract love." Always try to be as specific as you can for the best result.

Anointing Your Candle

You must next anoint your candle with oil. Vegetable oil is essential for this part, so don't use any other type of oil. Take your candle in one hand and apply some oil to a finger on your other hand. Starting at the top of the candle, run your finger in a straight line to the center of the candle. Then apply some more oil to your finger and start at the bottom of the candle, this time running your finger upward toward the center. While you are doing this, visualize your wish.

The Type of Candle to Use

You may need more than one candle per ritual, so it is better if you use small ones. By this, I do not mean those fashionable short, fat ones that are known as tea-light candles, but thin ones that are approximately the same size as a small cigar.

If you have any difficulty in obtaining them, try an Internet search. Failing that, you can use large tapered ones, but these can take as long as five hours to burn down, and it isn't safe to leave them unattended. It is essential during any ritual to allow your candle to burn down and go out of its own accord. If you extinguish the flame during a working spell, the spell will almost certainly fail.

Keep your stock of candles, matches, and lighters safely stored well out of reach of small children. All the usual precautions for matches and flammable objects should always be observed.

Angelic and Candle Influences

You must first say a prayer of protection over your lit candle. Some witches design their own protection prayer, and this really is the best method. As with any prayer, this will incorporate more meaning than a prayer from a book. As in everything to do with Wicca, such as altars, pentagrams, and spells, this should be personal to you.

A different angel represents each day of the week, so it is best to write seven short prayers. They can all be similar, but the angel's name should be included somewhere in the prayer. Following is a typical example of a protection prayer for a Sunday.

I summon thee Archangel Michael,

Ruler of the sun,

To enforce your magical energies and encircle protection

Around me during my work.

Send me your power and assist me at this time.

So mote it be.

Once you have written seven prayers for the seven days of the week, you can include them in your Book of Shadows so that you can use them every time that you start a spell. Remember that there is no right or wrong way to write these, because they don't have to be fancy or present too much of a challenge; you just need to be able to relate to them. If you get really stuck and can't find the words to write down, use the one I have written above, changing the angel's name with each day's prayer. I will show you the correspondences between the days of the week, their angels, and other features in a moment.

Before casting a spell, some witches like to perform a protective visualization. Some sit before their altar for five minutes or so with their eyes closed while imagining they are encircled by a purple light.

The more experienced witch may actually sit inside a drawn circle while casting her spell. This represents the "eternal circle of life," and while inside it, no harm can enter and none can go out either. This is an option that you can use, but I recommend that, by saying your initial prayer and meditating on positive thought, you will receive the greatest protection, and you will be able to go on to cast your spells in safety.

The Correspondences

The following are the features appropriate to each day of the week:

SUNDAY

Day:	Sunday
Angelic Ruler:	Archangel Michael
Planet:	The sun
Element:	Fire
Sign:	Leo
Colors:	Gold, orange, yellow
Incense:	Frankincense

Influences

- Anything relating to work, career, and ambitions
- Physical healing
- Personal money matters
- Self-confidence
- Sport
- Fatherhood

If you are worried about your health, the health of someone else, or if you are trying to overcome a lack of self-confidence, you should perform the ritual on a Sunday, recite your prayer for the day, and use a gold or yellow candle.

MONDAY

Day:	Monday
Angelic Ruler:	Archangel Gabriel
Planet:	The moon
Sign:	Cancer
Element:	Water
Colors:	Silver, blue
Incense:	Jasmine

Influences

- ☙ To increase psychic abilities
- ☙ Situations regarding the home and family
- ☙ Women, pregnancy, and motherhood
- ☙ Travel
- ☙ Secrecy

If someone whom you know is having trouble conceiving, you should perform the ritual on a Monday, recite your prayer for the day, and burn a silver or blue candle.

TUESDAY

Day:	Tuesday
Angelic Ruler:	Archangel Samuel
Planet:	Mars
Signs:	Aries, Scorpio
Element:	Fire
Color:	Red
Incense:	Pine

Influences

- Machinery, tools, and appliances

- Confidence, courage, and bravery

- Males

- Sexual energy and arousing passion

- Protection from violence—for example, muggers, rapists, and domestic abusers

If you are worried about your safety, you should perform your ritual on a Tuesday, recite the appropriate prayer, and use a red candle.

WEDNESDAY

Day:	Wednesday
Angelic Ruler:	Archangel Raphael
Planet:	Mercury
Signs:	Gemini, Virgo
Element:	Air
Colors:	Green, yellow
Incense:	Sandalwood

Influences

- Communication

- Education

- Concentration and memory

- Lost property

- Improving writing skills

- Travel by car or air

- Money, wealth, and work

- Physical attraction

Wednesday is the best day to perform money magic. If you are struggling with your finances, you should conduct your spell on a Wednesday, using the appropriate prayer and a yellow or green candle. Green is known to be powerful in connection with money magic.

THURSDAY

Day:	Thursday
Angelic Ruler:	Archangel Sachiel
Planet:	Jupiter
Signs:	Sagittarius, Pisces
Element:	Fire
Color:	Purple
Incense:	Cedar

Influences

- Wealth

- Gambling, speculating, and lotteries

- Political power

- Legal matters

- Success in business

If your business is failing, you should perform your ritual on a Thursday, recite your prayer for the day, and use a purple candle.

FRIDAY

Day:	Friday
Angelic Ruler:	Archangel Anael
Planet:	Venus
Signs:	Taurus, Libra
Element:	Earth
Colors:	Green, pink
Incense:	Jasmine

Influences

- Romance and love
- Attracting love
- Creating harmony in relationships and marriage
- Beauty
- Improving musical talents

Friday is the correct day for casting spells with love in mind, but should your Friday fall in a full moon phase, the results will be even more dynamic. If you need a romantic boost, you should perform your ritual on a Friday, recite the appropriate prayer, and use a green or pink candle. Pink is known to be extremely powerful for love spells, but red is used for passion.

SATURDAY

Day:	Saturday
Angelic Ruler:	Archangel Cassiel
Planet:	Saturn
Signs:	Aquarius, Capricorn
Element:	Earth
Colors:	Brown, black
Incense:	Myrrh

Influences

- The elderly

- Moving house and property matters

- The law of karma

- Inheritances and windfalls

- Self-discipline and concentration

- Peace of mind in confusing circumstances

- To stop harassment or bullying

If you need a positive outcome on a property move, you should perform your ritual on a Saturday, recite the appropriate prayer, and use a black or brown candle. Another variation, which is useful if your boss is being difficult, is to use a white candle to soften his mood.

10

Self-Defense

I t does no harm for us to cleanse and bless our home, keeping it free from any unpleasant energies that we might have absorbed from others or created ourselves. Even an argument between husband and wife can leave a heavy atmosphere, so it is always a good idea to clear it as soon as practicable, rather than to allow it to fester.

Mirrors

Mirror magic is a form of self-protection that every witch should learn right at the outset. If you think you may have an enemy or an adversary, it is best to act as swiftly and as promptly as you can, without tapping in to the darker side of occult practice.

Shop around and buy several small mirrors, the smaller the better. If you can't find small household mirrors, you can purchase a selection of compact makeup mirrors as an alternative. The objective is to place one mirror, facing outward, in each window of your home; then any negative influences that are being directed at you will reflect straight back to their original source threefold.

The mirrors work to banish and eliminate any evil, but because they are known to have originated from a natural substance that originated in the earth, they will also work as a sponge to absorb positive influences. That means that every time you send love and kindness out to others, the mirrors will also send it out, and you will receive love and kindness back. This is because the mirror will bounce the benefits back to their source, threefold. In this situation, everyone wins, so keep the mirrors in your windows at all times.

Some years ago, before I developed my present ability to judge character, there was a young woman whom I truly believed was my friend. She would be sweetness herself to my face, but spiteful behind my back. At the time, the thought crossed my mind that I may have been dealing with a "younger soul," but because I was more trusting back then, I dismissed the notion.

Unusual things started to happen in my home. After returning from her house one day, I came home to find that thousands of flying ants had invaded my kitchen. This woman's aged cat had died of cancer, and this naturally upset her. As it happened, two weeks prior to this I had acquired a beautiful tortoiseshell kitten for the children. It turned out that this "friend" was jealous of the kitten and resentful because she had lost her own cat. Ten days later—and in front of my children—the ironing board collapsed, crushing the poor animal and killing it. When I told her of our tragedy, I was stunned when she shrugged off the event as if it were unimportant.

Time passed, and I noticed that whenever my friend cooked for me, I would be violently sick. I started to watch while she was preparing food that was destined for me, but nothing seemed to be untoward; yet I was still vomiting after each meal. I began to think that it was all in my mind, so I turned to my spiritual guide for an answer.

I meditated for a few weeks, then, while dreaming, I became aware that my friend fancied my husband. This made no sense, as she was always keen to voice her dislike of him, and she frequently encouraged me to leave him. Some weeks later, I discovered that they had been sleeping together for some time! Partly due to this, I ended my marriage within the next year. After this, I discovered that the woman's father had been practicing the black crafts for over thirty years and that he had initiated her into this art. I was shocked at this knowledge, but now I see it as a being a valuable lesson that I needed to learn.

I was grateful to my guide for telling me of the affair, and I decided that one way to get her out of my life was to use mirror magic, so I put a tiny mirror in each window of my house. My intention was simply to get rid of her, but the mirrors turned her spite and hatred back on her. Within a week, her father became sick and was taken to hospital, and shortly afterward, her husband of thirteen years left her. Her life was torn to pieces.

The wickedness that these people had launched at me came back to them both threefold. Some might ask if I feel guilty about the outcome of mirror magic, but I didn't set out to hurt her or her father. I merely set out to protect my children, the beautiful innocent animals that I owned, and myself.

Salt

We see the salt cellar on our dinner table every night, but do any of us know the true significance of it and its meaning to a Pagan? For centuries, witches have considered sodium chloride (salt) a source of protection against evil. According to ancient folklore, salt was considered anathema to demons and witches working on the darker side of occult, thus capable of warding off the evil eye.

In the Middle Ages, it was believed that witches and the livestock around them could not consume anything salted. During the time of the witch hunts, the inquisitors who tortured or interrogated witches would protect themselves by wearing an amulet composed of salt and herbs that had been pressed into a wax disc and blessed on Palm Sunday. They considered that this would give them complete protection against the evil eye. One method of torture that they employed was forcing the supposed witch to eat a bowl of very salty food. They then denied the person access to water for many days, repeating the procedure and thus stepping up the torment.

Even to this day, there are many superstitions regarding salt. If we spill salt, we automatically take a pinch in our right hand and throw it over our left shoulder. At one time, salt was an expensive and important commodity, therefore spilling it would be considered a kind of sacrilege—literally like throwing money away, so by doing this little ritual, people brought the balance of good fortune back into their homes. Another belief was that if the devil decided to invade someone or come into his home, he would peer over the person's left shoulder. For some reason, spilled salt was a sign that the devil was around, so throwing some into his face was a way of banishing him.

If you sense there is an unpleasant and unhappy feel to your home or if someone you know is experiencing this—or even if you are moving into a new house—first light a white, lavender, or blue candle, then take it into each room of the dwelling. This simple ritualistic chant will start the magic.

Bless this house to bring harmony, light, and radiance.

Take away any negativity that is present and restore the balance

To one of love and peace.

So mote it be.

Once you have recited the incantation, throw a small teaspoon of salt across the room, then blow the candle out. To complete the cleansing procedure, this must be repeated in all the rooms of your home, using the same candle. You can carry out this process in your garden, using the same method. I have even known people who perform this ritual in their automobiles when they have had an accident or when they purchase a new car.

When you have been into every nook and cranny, leave the candle somewhere safe to burn all the way down and snuff itself out. You will notice a difference once you have done this. The home will feel lighter, have a calming influence, and any difficulties that you have will become less of a problem.

The Unicorn

Modern witches hold the unicorn dear to their hearts. This beloved animal is revered for its beauty, pure clarity, and spellbinding innocence. The unicorn is said to see no evil, and because of its purity, it is not permissible for any man to handle, harm, or entrap him.

In medieval history, this creature looked rather like a little one-horned goat, but now we see this fabulous animal as a white horse with golden hooves and a spiraled alicorn of gold. The mane and tail are allegedly spun from moonlight, and the unicorn will become visible only to those who believe in him.

The unicorn is resistant to poison, so tradition says that hunters would trap a unicorn, hack off the horn, and give it to the ruling monarch of the time. This would then be used to dip into his wine or food to save him from poisoning. Legend has it that if you wish to trap a unicorn, you must find a fair virgin who possesses only the purest of thoughts and take her to the depths of the forest. Then you must bind her to a tree, where she will remain until the unicorn comes to her to experience her love and tenderness.

Witches consider that keeping an image of a unicorn in the home acts as one of the highest forms of protection. I have a full-sized statue of a unicorn's head on the wall of my garden to protect all of the wildlife that comes to visit. I also have a white unicorn statuette in my house and a portrait of one hanging in my lounge. Mamma loves and treasures the unicorn so much that she has gone one step further and filled her entire bungalow with statues of them. At the last count, she had sixty-seven of them, and we have since renamed the house "The Stable"!

Angels

One of the best forms of protection is the angel. Any kind of angel will guard your home and watch over you. Ornamental angels or pictures of them are common in many homes throughout the world and among people of many different religions. Some witches wear little "angel on my shoulder" pendants for protection when out and about. However, angels in any form are a loving symbol of peace and well-being.

Colors

Colors symbolize the energies that we create in our homes. It is important for a witch to be surrounded by calm and tranquil shades, as it is known among witches that this is an aid to meditation and visualization.

I believe that colors can affect our moods. Have you ever visited a place where there are loud and garish furnishings? Some argue that they are cheerful influences, but spiritually minded individuals are sensitive to gaudy surroundings, and they find them depressing.

My eldest son was a very difficult and unsettled baby. He cried day and night, making sleep something that existed only in our memories. When he was born, I decorated his bedroom in bright yellow, blue, and red to make the nursery interesting and appealing. It looked very cheerful and inviting, but when I started to look into color therapy some months later, I decided to change the color scheme to a lilac pastel shade. Within two days, my baby was happily sleeping through the night.

For peace and comfort, decorate your home in gentle tints and shades. There is no specific color that you should go for; simply choose one that is easy on the eye. Two of the most psychic colors are blue and purple, so it is worth using these in any room that you use for psychic work or for meditation, as these colors are said to enhance and unleash your psychic abilities.

Another extremely psychic and spiritual color is turquoise. Astronauts have recorded that when traveling into space and looking down on our planet, it looks turquoise in color. Lemon and green will create a settled ambience, as does pale pink. Try to stay away from loud, daring schemes, such as reds and oranges. These colors cannot counteract unwanted or disconcerting influences and may make it hard for you to meditate. Brown, cream, beige, and similar shades are safe enough, but they are neutral and empty. Let your home say something about you, and fill it with as much peace and serenity as you can.

Let us move on to the subject of automobiles and their colors. Most men buy a vehicle for its style, performance, reliability, and speed. Women are less interested in these attributes—and in many cases, they look at the color before deciding to buy it. I know this doesn't relate to every woman, but almost all the women I have known consider the color of their automobile to be important.

Whether people know it or not, colors and their shades influence the way our life progresses, and they can influence certain situations that arise. Sounds weird, doesn't it? Have you ever heard someone complain that "Every red automobile I ever owned has been a nightmare" or "I've never had any luck with white vehicles"? I hear it all the time. Below I have listed some vehicle colors and their significance.

Red: If you drive a red vehicle, it is said that you prefer to live your life in the fast lane. Work and business issues tend to thrive, and this color also indicates new beginnings.

Blue: In England, statistics show that more blue automobiles crash every year than any other color. When driving a blue car, look out for oncoming traffic and don't expect to have much money in your wallet.

Yellow: A ray of sunshine. This color rarely gives a problem, and it will make its owner happy and contented.

Green: This is the color of money, so when you purchase a green vehicle, your money energy is said to double.

Black: This color can be problematic, and the vehicle will suffer mechanical problems. Although it may look snazzy, beware, because you may find that you have purchased an expensive item.

White: Said to be the purest of pure, although white automobiles can be a magnet for criminals. A friend of mine who knows the car trade says that this is because those who steal vehicles with the intention of selling them know that some of their "customers" might object to a vehicle of a particular color, while nobody seems have any objection to a white one. Hence, a white vehicle is easier for the criminal to sell.

Silver: Driven quite a lot by retired folk, as this symbolizes a time of peace and steadfastness. When driving a silver vehicle, the owner's life shouldn't be too challenging. This is another color that attracts wealth.

So the next time you are standing in the car dealership, deciding what make of vehicle you want, listen to your inner voice if it wants a red one or green one. It may just bring you luck!

11

Garden Magic

E veryone knows the enchantment of stepping into a beautiful garden and being surrounded by living nature, with the smells, sounds, and wonder of the seasons. Since the beginning of time, mankind has tried to improve on nature when making a garden. We have created formal gardens and special blooms, thus making many of the flowers and plants of today exquisite and unique.

Modern farming methods may increase the yield and even the size of individual vegetables, but this may remove some of the taste and nutritional elements. As for irradiated vegetables and genetically modified foods . . . well, perhaps it is best for me to stay off that subject. It saddens me, when walking around the supermarket, to see that there is rarely one carrot, turnip, or leek with a little honest, down-to-earth soil on it. Everything is so clinical and sterile. We buy our salads washed and prepared in little plastic bags, and our meat has been carefully prepared and prepackaged so that we hardly recognize the fact that it was once part of a living creature.

You will find many modern Wiccans rooting through the supermarket shelves for organic fruit and vegetables. I am fortunate enough to live in a beautiful, rural part of England with fields and cows all around me. This location is ideal for me as, being a true Taurean, I love to feel at one with nature.

One of my cherished childhood memories was when my grandfather, who owned an allotment [a communal garden plot], would bring home a wicker basket full to the brim with green peas in their pods. Mamma and I would sit in the sunshine and shell them into an ancient and battered colander. Nowadays, all we do is rip open a plastic bag from the freezer and shove the peas in a pan for fifteen minutes. We have lost the simple joy of growing, nurturing, and handling our food, but witches of both sexes strive hard to get back what we have lost.

I always have a windowsill full of herbs, and every year I supply my mamma and numerous friends with a large variety of these. I obviously have "idiot" written right across my forehead, because I do the work while they enjoy the results—but joking aside, it delights me to remain in close contact with such growing energies.

The magic of the garden has been recognized for many centuries. When we begin to create our garden, we are inadvertently interfering with nature as we try to tap into nature's forces and become one with our earth. This chapter shows the magical influences of some of the well-known living things that we can see around us.

Trees and Their Significance

ALDER

According to ancient folklore, this tree was well known as the tree of the fairies and sprites. If you sit or stand underneath it while meditating, it will enhance your psychic ability.

BEECH

If you have one of these in your garden, your life will prosper in an emotional and financial sense. Wrap your arms around a beech tree, and you will receive the prosperous energies that it sends out.

BIRCH AND OAK

It is said that the birch and the oak are husband and wife. Wherever the birch grows, the oak will be found nearby. A small cluster of birch leaves pinned to a woman's garment will ensure that she finds her true love and soul mate. A few oak leaves worn next to the heart is said to help it to work better.

CEDAR

The cedar tree will give you inner or outer strength. Hug a cedar to receive its properties.

CHERRY

This tree is so beautiful when in blossom that it is surprising that it carries a poor omen for marriages. If this tree grows in your garden, your relationship will be very stormy. Never bring cherry blossoms into the house before May, because you will find yourself quarrelling and arguing with loved ones. It is a good tree to have around for money energy, though—if you can bear the fighting!

CHESTNUT

The chestnut contains love energies. Put a few chestnuts on your altar for spells that are designed to stop your lover from straying.

CHRISTMAS TREE

This represents the winter solstice and New Year, so having a real tree at Christmastime symbolizes a new beginning. Always purchase a tree with the roots still attached, and when Christmas is over, plant it in your garden, as this brings good fortune.

If you throw away the tree, it reverses the effect. If you cannot plant the tree and decide to burn it or to burn any part of it, never do this before January 6, which is the twelfth night after Christmas, as to do so would bring misfortune.

ELDER

The elder holds incredible magical powers and helps witches with their work.

ELM

Carry the leaf of the elm in your pocket to restore self-esteem and dignity.

HOLLY TREE

A holly tree in your garden will bring luck, and it will also ward off evil spirits. Never burn holly branches until they are well and truly dead, as it is extremely unlucky to do so.

PLANE TREE

Place a few leaves from this tree on your altar when you are casting spells, as they will improve your brainpower.

POPLAR

This tree represents the lunar cycle and is known as the "tree of the waters."

ROWAN (MOUNTAIN ASH)

Should you be so fortunate as to have a rowan tree in your garden, then the land, people, and property are extremely blessed, as the fairies will reside nearby and protect the garden. It is said that this tree thrives and flourishes on land that was made sacred by ancient stone circles and Druid rites. Should the tree carry groups of red berries, then it is sure that a saintly soul is buried somewhere nearby.

WALNUT

The walnut represents hidden wisdom and fertility.

WILLOW

We all recognize the beauty of this tree, and its meaning is as enchanting as the tree itself, because it is thought to be sacred to the moon goddess. If you are lucky enough to own a willow, the moon goddess herself will bless you.

Flowers and Their Significance

BRYONY

When spellcasting to ease premenstrual syndrome or rheumatic complaints, place a few bryony leaves on your altar, as this will heal and restore.

CARNATION

The meaning of the carnation varies from country to country. In traditional English folklore, carnations were used to enhance love spells. The colors were significant, as red was for passion, pink was for pure love, and yellow was used to reject an unwanted suitor. In other European countries, the carnation became associated with death and funerals.

CLOVER

We all know the luck a four-leaf clover can bring, so finding one is a wonderful omen, promising a prosperous future. To be given a clover means that you will soon hear good news.

DAISY

The little flower of innocence. Place on your altar when performing spells for the well-being of children.

FOXGLOVE

 This is a plant that is best left alone and avoided: it contains digitalis, which can cause serious heart problems.

IRIS

This flower holds the power of light. Place it on your altar when casting spells for depression. This really works well!

JASMINE

This is a terrific flower for attracting a lover. Either wear the perfume, or cast a spell while burning jasmine incense.

LILY

This has been known throughout time as the flower of peace. If your life is a hive of activity and you require some peace and quiet, place a lily on the altar to bring tranquility.

MARIGOLD

If you suspect that your partner is being unfaithful, take a few petals from this flower when the moon is full, and carry them on your person until the petals wither. Once they have done so, you will know the truth. (This takes great courage!)

PANSY

This flower enhances meditation. It also helps you to contact loved ones who have passed over. Sleep with a few petals under your pillow.

PRIMROSE

Place on the altar when spellcasting for troublesome teenagers. It helps to settle adolescent minds.

SUNFLOWER

This flower works well if you want to cast a spell to ward off infatuation. Place this on the altar during spellcasting.

TULIP

Carry the petals of a tulip on your person to attract the lover you want.

VALERIAN

! Valerian grows best in rainy areas where the soil is acid. Although a wild flower, it is also considered to be a herb—and in this case, a herb that is associated with the god, Mercury.

In astrology, Mercury rules the nervous system, so Valerian would seem to be a good plant to use for anxiety and sleeplessness. It is a fact that, in this instance, myth matches up with reality, so it is not surprising to find ground Valerian root available in capsule form in natural-health shops.

If you take Valerian, keep rigidly to the stated dose, because it can be dangerous in large quantities. **Never give it to children or your pets.** If you add it to bathwater, use no more than two capsules, because it is not a good idea to absorb too much Valerian through the skin.

VIOLET

When conducting a health spell, place some violets on the altar, and this will help to restore health. It is also known to represent true love, either in the sense of the love you wish to attract or in your own feelings for someone else.

Creatures and Their Significance

ANT

Ants are intelligent little creatures that lead busy lives. You should try not to kill them. If they nest in your house or garden, when the moon is waning, just ask them to leave. Stand over the ants, asking them kindly but firmly to move on. Do this for three nights.

If this fails, and you end up with a colony of them in your kitchen cupboard, you have my permission to buy ant powder and lay the ants to rest.

BADGER

The badger is said to possess supernatural power. Should you be so fortunate as to see one, your property is likely to have special supernatural energies or ley lines running through it, because the badger is greatly attracted to these.

Mamma has a family of badgers that visit her on a regular basis; hence, no food is ever wasted in her house. Farmers are convinced that this creature transmits bovine tuberculosis, so it may be worth checking out how your local farmers feel about badgers before you encourage them too much.

BAT

Should a bat fly in a circle over your house or garden, any spell-craft is sure to work, as they predict the witching hour.

BEE

These are the little priests of our gardens, and they are one of our most treasured creatures. We should always respect bees, as they are said to foretell the future. They cannot abide swearing or bad language of any kind, so never curse in front of a bee.

It is lucky to have a bee in your house. Should it fly around a baby's cradle, the child will have incredible luck and protection for the rest of his or her life. If a bee flies into your hand, it will bring an abundance of wealth. Once again, common sense is needed here, because some people are so allergic to bee stings that they can fall into anaphylactic shock and die after just one sting.

CAT

For centuries, cats have been considered the witches' familiar. Whether an average tabby or more finely bred, a cat possesses psychic powers and can read the thoughts of its owner. It takes a special person to understand the spirit of the cat, so if you happen to be a cat fan, then you are reaching toward a higher vibration.

People who despise cats are shallower by nature and may have many reincarnations to come. I recently read a popular psychology book that talked about the differences between men and women. One of the comments in the book that made me laugh was that women love to feed, soothe, and stroke cats, while men tend to kick them whenever the woman is not looking.

DRAGONFLY

To see a dragonfly means that things will start to happen quickly in your life and a whirlwind time is ahead, so get ready!

FLY

Flies are not popular creatures for obvious reasons. They do not represent good things and are best kept out of the house. If you have a fly in the house, ask it nicely to leave, but if all else fails, feel free to use the fly spray.

FROG

Another lucky creature. See a frog in the garden, and you are sure to prosper. If you see a dead frog or if you run over one, news of death will follow.

GRASSHOPPER

Come face to face with a grasshopper, and you will be sure to travel soon.

HARE

This is the lunar animal, and it has the attributes of all moon deities. It represents rejuvenation and intuition. The earlier Pagan meaning was that the hare represented fertility and the opening of spring. Many true witches keep a symbol of a hare somewhere in their homes.

LADYBIRD

This insect may be more familiar as a ladybug or even a maybug to American readers. The ladybird is said to be the fairy's pet. To have a ladybird land on you is very lucky. Make a wish before the ladybird flies away, and your wish is sure to come true.

MOLE

It is lucky to find a molehill, though it is not so lucky for your lawn. Place an upright glass bottle into the hole and the mole will move on—then use some of the fresh soil the mole has dug for your plant potting.

RABBIT

This is another lunar creature. To have a wild rabbit in your garden means that you will hear of a pregnancy, or you may become pregnant yourself.

RAT

Sadly, the rat gets a bad press, and its meaning isn't much better. To see a rat means news of a death.

SPIDER

Many of us are afraid of spiders, but ancient folklore held that the spider is very sensitive to humans, and that if you talk to a spider, it will understand you. A spider in the house promises prosperity and happiness. If one falls on you from above, then money luck is predicted. If one runs over your clothes, it will bring beautiful new garments. Catching a spider and putting it in your pocket for a few seconds, without hurting it, will make money come in abundance.

SQUIRREL

Although loved by many, if seen in your garden, a squirrel could mean that someone around you is deceiving you or telling you lies.

WASP

This is another little creature that we dislike—and with good reason. To be stung by a wasp is not only painful, it is also considered to be a warning that you must be on your guard over jealousy or someone who is wishing you ill.

WORM

Kill a worm by accident, and news of an accident will follow.

Birds and Their Significance

There are many superstitions about these creatures, and although I love them, they can worry me, because I am very superstitious. In the north of England, a bird that accidentally flies into a house, or even seeing a bird that is kept as a pet, suggests that news of a death is on the way. It is said that wild birds are the messengers of the animal kingdom.

BLACKBIRD

A member of the crow family that is reputed to bring luck. Should she stand and sing to you, love will shortly enter your life.

CROW

To see a crow is fortunate. Speak to the bird, and your wisdom will grow.

CUCKOO

If you hear the cuckoo sing in spring, make a wish, and it will surely be granted. If you hear her while you are standing on grass, then wealth will come your way during the following year.

FINCH

These little birds are a good omen. Tell them your problems, and they will fly away with them, so that your difficulties will soon disappear.

MAGPIE

This bird is not liked very much, but I happen to like it. To see a single magpie is said to be a bad omen. Say the word "raven" to counteract any bad luck. To see two magpies is a good omen. The rhyme about magpies that follows is an ancient British one that many children still sing:

One for sorrow

Two for joy

Three for a girl

Four for a boy

Five for silver

Six for gold

Seven for a secret

Never to be told.

OWL

The owl is known as the fortune-teller. Ask the owl a question, and one hoot means "no," while two hoots mean "yes." More than two hoots mean you must ask your question again.

PHEASANT

If you see a pheasant on your property, and if children live in the house, they will always be protected from life's dangers.

PIGEON

Should one land on your lawn, you could hear of an infidelity.

ROBIN

This delightful bird is considered to be a sign of death, so you may hear of a death after seeing a robin. It is possible that the idea of death comes from the fact that English robins are most visible in the dead of winter when nothing is growing.

SPARROW

A friendly little bird, but should he fly into your house, news of a serious illness or a death will follow.

SWALLOW

Should this bird nest in your eves, your property will be protected from storms and blizzards.

WOODPECKER

This bird possesses magical powers and is said to be the guardian of kings and trees.

Other Garden Meanings

ACORN

The acorn is a symbol of life.

Would you like to know if you and your lover will marry? If so, take two acorns and stand under the full moon. Give one your name and the other the name of your lover, then drop them into a bowl of water. If the acorns float toward each other, you will be united in marriage; if they sail apart, the relationship will fail.

BAY LEAF

In cultures across the world, there are people who understand that the bay leaf carries extensive healing properties.

If you are feeling unwell, tired, or in need of energy, take one teaspoon of crushed bay leaves in a cup of boiling water to restore and refresh your vitality. European witches hang a few bay leaves above their front door to ward off evil.

GARLIC

If taken orally, garlic can relieve the symptoms of colds and flu. You can hang a garlic bulb inside the exterior doors of your property, as this will afford your home added protection by warding off evil.

HEATHER

Heather hanging in the window also protects the house from unwanted energies.

MISTLETOE

Precious mistletoe growing in your garden is believed to bring peace and protection to your abode.

We have a huge spray growing from our apple tree, and we distribute it to all our neighbors at Christmastime.

WHITE FEATHER

When you find a white feather on the ground, this is a sign from your guardian angel that you are being protected.

And Finally ... the Original Meaning of Easter

Educated Christians will not argue the fact that Easter started out as a Pagan festival, and because of this, some are averse to celebrating it at all.

Religious historians have discovered that the Easter/Pagan connection dates back to a time when Cybele, the Phrygian fertility goddess, was believed to have a companion named Attis, who was born via a virgin birth. He was said to have died and then to have been been resurrected every year between the days of March 22 and 25.

It is assumed that Christians absorbed these resurrection legends when they attempted to convert the Pagans. Realizing that it would be tricky to convert Pagans from their ancient way of life, they adopted the festival as their own and altered the story slightly, making it more fitting to the new Christian religion.

Easter derives from the ancient goddess of dawn named Eostre, meaning "moving toward the rising sun." Other names for her throughout the world are Eostra, Eostar, Eostrae, Estre, Eastre, and Easter. Derivatives from these names are also estrus and estrogen. In the Pagan and Wiccan faiths, Easter falls on the Sunday following the first full moon after the spring equinox in March.

Nature-loving Pagans rejoice in the coming of the spring, which is when the bleakness and cold of the winter is passing away, and the buds start to bloom, representing rebirth and new life. It is interesting to consider the word "estrogen," as we know this is a hormone that is connected to human fertility. The hare and the egg were considered to be symbols of fertility, so these were worshipped as part of the spring festival.

It is fascinating to see that we still give chocolate hares and eggs to our children today, also treating them to Easter bunny toys. Do people ever consider that by doing this, they are actually celebrating a Pagan festival in a Pagan manner? Do they also realize that this was considered to be the start of the year in Roman times, and the reason for Aries being the first sign of the zodiac?

12

Amulets, Talismans, and Other Magical Methods

Amulets and talismans are different names for the same thing. They are symbolic emblems that have illustrations or inscriptions on them, and when they are "charged," they help their owners achieve their desires.

Amulets can be made from any natural thing, such as fine wood chips and small wooden blocks, or from stones, rocks, or finely polished metal disks. The amulet needs an illustration or description imbedded into it that represents the thing that the owner requires. Some carry an image on one side and a written inscription on the reverse. Amulets, talismans, and charms are not confined to witches. Indeed, male, non-Pagan individuals carry a lucky charm around with them when they feel the need for it or if they feel that they might be in any kind of danger. Many will choose to carry a particular image without realizing the power it portrays or its Pagan significance.

If you carve or inscribe the amulet yourself, this will increase its power and give better results. You don't need to be a brilliant artist to engrave or draw a picture on an amulet, because it will work well however you do it. You can chisel, draw, or paint your chosen symbol. It is quite acceptable to make or design an amulet for someone else—with his or her permission, of course. If you do this, not only do you need to believe in your magic, but the person you are doing it for also needs to understand what you are doing and believe in its properties as well. Added to a ritual, this can help to produce a positive outcome.

When I was in my early twenties, a lady who was desperate to conceive came to see me. After many years of trying, and in spite of everything she did, she still remained barren. I toyed with the idea of performing a spell for her, but I decided to create an amulet instead, because it had been a long time since I had had the satisfaction of making one of these wonderful items.

While I was creating it, I entered a positive thinking mode. I created an amulet from a small stone that I had picked up on the beach some months before. I used enamel to paint a figure of a pregnant woman on one side and the name of the lady on the reverse. While making the amulet, I concentrated intently on the idea of the woman becoming a mother. When the amulet was ready, I charged the stone on my altar and then gave it to her with instructions for her to keep it on her person at all times.

Magic sometimes doesn't work in the way we would like it to. In this instance, I couldn't help laughing, because she telephoned me six weeks later to say that she still hadn't managed to conceive, but her treasured pet cat had! Sometime later, she was the proud owner of three kittens that she subsequently mothered like crazy.

You can't always change the laws of destiny, and it was not hers to be a parent in this lifetime—but the amulet had certainly done its job for one whose fate it was.

You need to charge your amulet, and this can be done in a variety of ways. If your object is solid and made from metal, wood, or stone, an appropriate method of cleansing and charging can be by way of placing the amulet in a stream for a few minutes. It will then absorb the natural forces of life and draw their strength and power into itself. Naturally, you will need to use a different method if you have made your amulet from paper. Paper is a good substance for those who need a quick and effective charm. Place your amulet in the middle of your pentagram on your altar. A simple five-minute ritual will get it up and running.

Designing and Charging an Amulet

If you want to make a quick and easy amulet, you will need some sturdy paper. Cut this into your choice of shape, something that will fit inside a wallet or pocket. When you have done this, set out your altar with your pentagram in the center and your amulet sitting comfortably in the middle of it.

Light two white candles. Sit very quietly in front of your altar, focusing all of your energies on the amulet before you. Focus intensely on it, soaking up every detail that you created. Take the amulet in your left hand (the hand closest to your heart) and imagine that a brilliant white light surrounds you. Keep your eyes firmly fixed on the amulet and visualize its future purpose.

If money is the problem, visualize yourself paying your bills with ease. If you want a new job, imagine the kind of job or the specific company that you want to work for. If you are doing this correctly, you will actually be able to see the light from the candle charging your amulet. At this point, you should get a strong feeling of emotional comfort and security. You may feel slightly light-headed, but don't worry; this is quite normal. Next place the amulet on your pentagram in front of the lit candle, and look directly at the burning flame. Repeat the following invocation:

I summon thee, angels of the cosmos,

To bring magical power to the symbol before me.

Clear it of negative and cleanse it with positive.

Let it shine forever.

So mote it be.

Leave the amulet on the altar for about half an hour, letting the candles burn merrily away; then your amulet will be charged. If you find that for some reason your amulet isn't working for you, or your situation hasn't improved, then recharge it in the same way. Once charged properly, the process shouldn't need to be repeated again; but it may not always work the first time, so be prepared to do it a second time if necessary.

All spells and magical methods work best if they are kept secret. I have quite a collection of amulets and decided that I needed a permanent home for them, so I decorated a small box in which to keep them. I charge them first and then leave them untouched until I feel the need to use one.

If you decide to use a box, find one that is large enough to hold about twelve amulets—for instance, something the size of a chocolate box would be ideal. Your next task is to hunt for about six stones. The best would be those that you find in the garden or pick up from the ground or the beach. Don't buy fancy stones, because you will need those that possess the properties and energies of the earth, so raw stones that have not been touched are ideal.

There are many ancient inscriptions that you will find in books, but it is best to design your own amulets, thus making them completely personal to you. Amulets are fun and inexpensive, and when charged properly, they really do work.

Lucky Charms

Most people possess a lucky charm at some point in their lives. These are objects that are believed to enhance your life in some way or to bring you luck and good fortune. They are very similar to amulets and talismans; but whereas amulets tend to be descriptive, charms tend to be more personal to the owner.

Some people keep a lucky penny, a soft toy, a four-leaf clover, or gemstones. The list is endless. Not many actually know how the charm works, but they believe in it nonetheless, and they carry it with them when they go to job interviews or on any other occasion that may need some extra luck.

Charms work because the owner subconsciously charges the object by believing in its magic. If the individual knew how to charge the charm correctly, it would do even better for them. By charging the item in a similar way to charging your pentagram or amulet, the charm becomes personal to you. By believing in it, you are inadvertently transporting the energy and magic directly to the charm.

If you don't already own a lucky charm, look around the shops and purchase something small enough to carry with you when you are in need of a bit of luck. There are no rules attached to acquiring this object, because you only need to like it, but once it's safely in your care, try charging it.

CHARGING A CHARM

Place your charm in the center of your pentagram. It will automatically gain strength from this and from the altar. Bless and anoint five small white candles. Place a candle on each of the five points of the pentagram and light them. Sit in front of your altar and recite the following:

Archangels of the universe, bring power to this object before me;

Send your vibration and enhance the luck that it possesses.

Work this magic for me today.

So mote it be.

Whenever you need some extra luck, carry your charm with you, and things should improve. Over the years, you may find that you acquire quite a few charms, so it's a nice idea to house them properly. Find yourself a fancy box to keep them in; alternatively, pop them in with your amulets.

Verbal Rituals

Repetitive chanting can be a successful method of performing verbal spells. When I want something really badly, I chant or sing the name of the thing, over and over again. If someone were to eavesdrop while I was doing this, they would think I had gone soft in the head. Mostly I try to avoid being overheard, but even if someone does inadvertently overhear me—well, it works, so what the heck!

This exercise can be a time-saver, because once you have the knack, there will be less necessity for you to rush to your altar every time you need to carry out a spell. You can chant away to your heart's content while doing some chore that doesn't require mental concentration. Verbal rituals work in a similar way to candle rituals. Some of these rituals require you to recite an invocation seven times—in a similar way to candle rituals, but without the candle. For example, when I need to drive somewhere and my automobile is packed to the brim with dogs and children, I say the protection prayer of the day in my head and silently focus on this before starting my journey. I have even used this on occasion when my auto refused to start.

You need to shut yourself off from the situation around you for a few moments if you want to obtain the best results. A parent who is trying to get a meal ready when her children are arguing with each other can shut out the noise of a harmless squabble, so you can also shut out the world for a few moments when you need to. In short, this concentration on what you need is a kind of mind-over-matter technique that brings results.

There are situations during which you can use your mind to influence others. Try this example. One day when you are sitting in a restaurant or when you are traveling on a train, stare intently at the back of some stranger's head and focus your mind on them. It won't be long before they turn around to see who wants them! Here is a story that shows the opposite, which is not so much how to attract someone's attention as how to divert it.

One day during my youth, I went to a disco club with some girlfriends. A man who was frankly dreadful decided that I was to be his catch of the night. For over an hour this crude, uncouth man persisted in trying to talk to me. I made several excuses and tried to walk away from him, but each time he grabbed my arm or followed me. I finally escaped to the safety of the ladies' room and spent the regulation young woman's half hour or so rearranging my face and hair in the mirror. When I emerged—the man was lying in wait and sporting a big smile.

Not being the confident and assertive woman I am today, I put up with this. Looking back on the situation from the distance of time, I realize that I should have called the security man or asked one of my friends to help me out. But I decided to banish him with magic. I calmly looked down at my feet and silently willed him over and over again to go away. For a while, the man continued to harass me, then all of a sudden he shook my hand and said he had to leave. To this day, I swear that Mr. Obnoxious had no idea what happened, or why. If you do this kind of thing, it must be because you really need something, and it must never be to wish someone ill will.

When you become an experienced witch, you will be able to conduct some spells without a candle. Instead of physically lighting it, you will be able to visualize yourself lighting it, and then you can say your prayer of protection and recite your ritual in the usual way. Obviously, your spell is likely to be more effective with the use of an actual candle, but this alternative method does come in handy on some occasions. Try something like this when simple things aggravate you—for example, if you want to get rid of a neighbor who has outstayed his or her welcome. Do be careful though, because once you have mastered this technique, your thoughts will become like missiles.

THE MIND-OVER-MATTER RITUAL

Sometimes we need to fix an immediate situation, but we haven't the time to perform a long-winded ritual. The following will suit almost any quick-fix situation.

Bless, anoint, and inscribe a small white candle in the usual way. Place the candle directly in the center of your pentagram. Alternatively, bless, anoint, and inscribe five small white candles and place one on each point of the pentagram. Next, say your protection prayer for the day over the lit candle or candles. Think about what it is that you want, and imagine your wish being reality. Then ask for what you want nine times. For instance, if your car won't start, try the following:

I desire for the car to start

I desire for the car to start

I desire for the car to start

I desire for the car to start

I desire for the car to start

I desire for the car to start

I desire for the car to start

I desire for the car to start

I desire for the car to start

So mote it be

Believe that your desire will be accomplished, and you will find that the spell works. However, it is not a good idea to become lazy and use this method for everything, because when you need to do something thoroughly, you will find that you have forgotten the proper procedure.

An Unusual Use for Electrical Appliances

Several years ago, I was busy in the kitchen, but my mind was on the fact that I needed to get into contact with someone fairly urgently. I broke every rule in the book and simply lit a candle, placing it on the top of the microwave oven while defrosting a chicken. Focusing my mind on the person, I mentally asked them to contact me. Within a short space of time, the phone rang, and my friend was on the line.

I put this down to coincidence, but sometime later I did the same thing again—with the same result. I discussed this with Mamma, and we came to the conclusion that the proximity of the candle to an electrical appliance that was doing something at the time might just have accelerated the magic. Silly? Perhaps so. However, we tested the system many times and with many different electrical appliances and it always worked. This might come in handy for people at work, where you can't rush home to use your altar. You could try this with the photocopier or on some other electrical appliance while it is in action.

It is not a good idea to use your computer as an altar or to do anything magical when in close proximity to it, because this will make the computer go wrong. There may be people around who find it hard to believe in the power of magic, but computers are more sensitive than humans are, and they will definitely go haywire in response to the power of magic. If your computer is acting up for no good reason (even without having been in the close proximity of magical acts), treat it to one of those pink quartz stones that are sold in spiritual shops and gift shops. Place this on the part of the computer that houses the "works," and you will quickly notice that this will calm your machine, and it should prevent further problems.

13

Preparing Yourself for Spellcasting

Some people love the idea of meditating, others think that it will be boring or a waste of time. The fact is that you won't get anywhere with your spellcasting if you can't attune yourself, so the following easy meditation techniques will begin to turn your mind, your psyche, and your aura in the right direction for the work that you wish to do.

Before you begin to cast spells, you must try to clear your mind and thoughts and rid yourself of any negative vibrations. Now let us take a look at meditation and visualization. It is important to focus when you perform ritualistic tasks, because you need to master the art of tuning in to your inner self so that the spells that you use will be effective.

When someone begins to learn the art of meditation, they usually follow the guidelines written in certain books or teachings. This is fine as a beginner's guide, but as you progress, you will form your own methods and exercise your own techniques. There are many different ways to meditate, and I am sure that you will eventually discover the system that suits you best. What suits you may not work for another person, but as long as you practice regularly, you will find you can really can tap into your subconscious and become at one with yourself.

Meditation and visualization are not only useful for putting yourself into the right frame of mind for performing rituals, but they are also a fantastic sleep aid. I read somewhere that ten minutes of good meditation is equivalent to four hours sleep, so it really is worth giving it a try. I usually advise my students to spend a couple of weeks working on their meditation before starting to cast spells.

How to Meditate

Find a quiet place in your home. It is probably best to lie down on your bed, but relaxing in a scented tub can create the perfect setting. Take care, because meditation can make you sleepy; so for goodness sake don't drown! Surround yourself with scented candles. Ensure that you have complete peace and quiet and that your family and pets are unlikely to disturb you.

Take three deep breaths and clear your thoughts as you do so. In your mind, recite your protection prayer for whatever day of the week it happens to be and imagine that you are looking out through your inner eye. Keep your breathing steady as you do this. In your mind, count down from thirty to zero. Your body should start to feel light, floaty, and relaxed at this point.

Next, take ten deep breaths, but this time, imagine that with every inward breath you are inhaling all the magical energies of the universe. As you exhale, imagine that you are ejecting the negativity that is within you. This is called spirit purification, and if performed properly, it can give you a wonderful sense of well-being. The next stage is to take a further ten deep breaths, letting the magic that you have allowed in to envelope your spirit. It takes practice to perfect this, so don't be too disappointed if you fall asleep; enjoy the rest and try again the following night.

HOW DO YOU KNOW IF YOU'RE DOING IT RIGHT?

This is a good question, but it is worth mentioning that every individual will experience something different. Many people discover that when in deep meditation, they see colors and shapes appearing in a whirling motion behind their closed eyelids. When this happens to me, I know that I am meditating properly. Some describe feelings of total numbness or feel they are just about to astrally project. Others may only be aware of feeling extremely relaxed.

Let's assume that you have mastered meditation and are feeling completely tranquil; you have cleared your thoughts, and you are ready to visualize your need. Initially, focus your mind on what it is that you want, remembering that a thought is a living energy and that you are projecting that energy outward. Concentrate entirely on what you need—whether it is work, money, good health, love, or anything else. You should envisage this for as long as you can—usually around five to ten minutes is sufficient.

Next, gradually begin to clear your mind again, this time counting upward from zero to thirty, keeping your breathing as steady as before. After this, your meditation or visualization will be complete and you can go back to your normal everyday life.

Although this has nothing to do with meditation, it is interesting to note that if you use this technique and then set out to see a person's aura, you will find that you can do so. Sit your subject in front of a plain background and stare at their head and shoulders for a while and then close your eyes.

While your eyes are closed, you will see the outline of the person in grey or black. This is due to their shape being temporarily imprinted on your retina. However, you will soon begin to see colors swirling around the head and shoulders of this imprinted image. Try opening your eyes again and staring for a few more moments, then close them again; this time, the colors of the person's aura will be even clearer. This technique is called seeing with the third eye.

Start to Cast Spells

If you have charged your pentagram and set your altar in place, blessed and prepared your candles, and if the moon in the right phase and your meditation is perfected, you are ready to start performing rituals.

It is important to walk before you can run, so I will give you a couple of simple spells to begin with. Try not to skip pages or turn to the more interesting spells that come later in this book. Keep in mind the importance of taking everything a step at a time for a satisfactory result.

A SPELL TO CREATE POSITIVE ENERGY IN THE HOME

It is important to make your home a peaceful sanctuary for your-self and for those who visit. It is best to perform this spell once a month to keep the home clean and free from disturbance. This is like a giving the home a spiritual spring cleaning.

Day:	Begin on a Sunday
Moon phase:	Any
Candles:	Seven different candles that are the colors of the rainbow
Ribbons:	Seven colored ribbons to match the seven candles
Also:	Make a flower arrangement—this can be real or artificial

• Tie each ribbon in a bow around the bottom of the matching colored candle, then place the candles in suitable candle holders.

• Put the flower arrangement in or near the window and then place the candles in front of the flowers. Use common sense, and avoid placing the candles so close to artificial flowers or drapes that they could be a fire hazard.

• Light the candles for fifteen minutes each day, blowing them out when the time is up. Do this every day until the candles are so worn down that there is nothing left to work with.

This simple spell works as a spiritual cleansing or blessing to the property and can generate positive energy all around the home and the people living there.

A SPELL TO CHANGE YOUR LUCK FOR THE BETTER

I have chosen this spell because most people could do with a bit of extra luck in their lives. If you are already lucky enough, you can conduct the spell for another person who might need a change of fortune.

This spell works almost immediately, and it brings about a positive energy that will improve difficult circumstances.

Day: Begin on a Sunday
Moon phase: Any, but avoid the dark of the moon
Candles: Use a white candle, preparing it as before by blessing and anointing it

- Inscribe the name of the person and the words "good fortune" on the candle.

- Place the candle in the center of your pentagram on your prepared altar.

- Light the candle and sit quietly, envisaging you or the other person being happy and trouble free.

- Recite the protection prayer you wrote for Sunday, summoning the Archangel Michael.

- Recite the following seven times with meaning, adapting the wording accordingly when speaking the person's name:

I desire to enhance [name]'s luck,

And to be successful in all that he/she does,

Bring forth the good and banish the bad.

[Say this seven times, then say:]

So mote it be.

If you were performing the spell for yourself, you would follow the instructions above, but word it as follows:

I desire to enhance my luck,

And to be successful in all that I do.

Bring forth the good and banish the bad.

[Say this seven times, then say:]

So mote it be.

Remember to use a new candle that has been properly prepared on each of the seven days. On each occasion, let the candle burn all the way down and put itself out. If you find that your luck has changed for the better after three or four days, don't abandon the spell.

This technique is rather like taking a course of antibiotics, because you have to finish the course or the problem could return. Carry on for the full seven days, and your ritual will be complete. Finally, please remember to keep an eye on what the moon is doing so that you don't run into the time of the dark of the moon.

14

Spells for Money, Business, and Your Career

On many occasions when I come across someone who doesn't understand the way that the world of spirit or magic works, they will ask me why I haven't won the national lottery or why I don't live in the lap of luxury. This is a good question, and it is not an easy one to answer.

The first rule seems to be that you have to really *need* the money, rather than just fancy having it. Some years ago, I tried performing a spell that would net me 10 million dollars, which was the amount on offer in that week's lottery. So, I carefully inscribed $10 million on my candle and went ahead with the spell. I won $100! I was delighted with my win and realized that this was the amount of money that I needed—and not the amount that I fancied having.

Some witches feel that it is so wrong to perform money spells that they absolutely refuse to do so. First, we need to recognize that money is a form of energy. If it is your destiny to be wealthy, then you will be, but you may have other disappointments to cope with. Our lives are a form of education, and if it is our lot to be poor, then we will be. Having said this, I don't believe that we should suffer unnecessarily, so if you want to keep the wolf from the door, do try some money spells.

The arguments about spirituality and money tend to rage around me. For instance, there are many people who consider that it isn't ethical to charge for giving Tarot readings. They say that psychic ability or the knack of being able to read the Tarot is a gift and that it should be freely given to others.

Musical talent, the ability to act, sing, dance, tell jokes, kick a football, win at tennis, and much more are also gifts. These people expect to be paid (often extremely well) for their ability to excite and entertain others, so why shouldn't we expect to be paid for the time that we give to others? My accountant has an aptitude for working with figures, but he hasn't yet offered to do my books for nothing!

In short, we have to pay other people for their services or products, so we have to earn the money with which to do that in the first place. In Norse mythology, the god Odin says that a gift must always be repaid by a gift, so a client could suffer from bad luck if he doesn't give something in exchange. So, if you want a reading from a psychic, be prepared to pay something for it.

Having said this, there is a fine line that exists here; I wouldn't necessarily charge someone for lighting a candle and saying a few words on their behalf. If I wanted to nitpick, I could ask a person to pay for the candle, but that would be all. However, if someone decides that they want to pay me for doing this small thing, I am likely to pass the money on to a charity or to someone who badly needs it. So let us leave the subject of ethics for now and see how we can improve your finances and also the financial situations of those who consult you.

If you really are feeling the pinch financially and want a bit of help, do not ask for more than you need. If performed correctly, the spell will work, and you will receive some cash within a few days. When this happens, take a small portion of the money and give it away as a way of saying thank you to the "universe." It doesn't have to be a large sum; a modest amount is fine. If you're greedy and keep the entire amount for yourself, it's likely that something will happen to make you lose the lot. Remember my story of winning $100 on the lottery? Well, foolishly, I kept the lot, and I was faced with an unexpected and very hefty dental bill a week later.

Money magic works best when your funds are very low, and you don't know how you're going to pay for something that is essential. At such times, get out your candles, and don't feel guilty about it. The results can be almost immediate, but they may not necessarily come into view in the way that you envisage. The following is an example of what I mean.

A long-standing client who ran an extremely successful healing center came to me some years ago and asked me for a Tarot reading. Although I didn't know her very well, I had recommended her to some of my other clients, because although she had not been in the business long, she had built up a good reputation.

Her premises were in the heart of town, making them easily accessible, but the owner of the property that she was renting had decided to sell up. He gave her first refusal to buy the place, and she had tried every avenue to raise the money. However, owing to a previous bad debt situation, she couldn't get help from a bank or any other such organization. It would have been impossible for her to find another place that was as convenient to her type of business as this one was.

Feeling very low, she came to me in a last-ditch attempt to see if the cards could predict what would happen and offer some guidance. Even though she was going through a tough time, I had quite a good feeling about the whole thing, so I gave her a simple candle spell to perform at home.

About five days had passed when she telephoned me. She was almost hysterical, so at first I found it hard to make any sense of what she was saying. When she had finally composed herself, she told me that a check for quite a large amount had dropped onto her mat that morning. Apparently, she had taken out some insurance when she was married to her first husband, and, after being tied up for years, the policy had finally reached maturity. She had totally forgotten about this insurance. The lady was caught between weeping and laughter; since then, her interest in spell-casting has grown, and she now casts spells on a regular basis.

There are many stories like this that I could tell you, although most are not as dramatic as this one. It is important to bear in mind that if the desire is legitimate and if the spirit world wishes you to follow a specified route, the funds will be provided and the doors opened for you to step through.

There are other forms of magic apart from candle magic that will help with financial matters, and the following traditions have been known to improve finances and add a little more weight to a purse.

Folklore Traditions

To attract money, keep a small piece of string in your purse or wallet. When times are hard, you should never be without it. If you own a shop or business, keep a piece of string in your cash register or a small magnet in your shop.

Should you see a penny or money of any sort in the street or on the ground, pick it up and keep it in your pocket for nine days. Never walk away from it, because it is meant for you. I expect you have heard the expression "finders, keepers"; well, this is also an old folklore tradition. If you should come across a roll of bank notes tumbling down the street, though, it's probably best to call the police. Doing a good deed like this acts in a positive manner, and you are likely to receive good fortune in another way as a result.

If you drop a coin, however small, never leave it on the ground, because that symbolizes throwing money away. By ignoring the cash, you will soon lose money.

Another old idea was to keep a small magnet in your purse or wallet, but a magnet will spoil your credit cards, so perhaps just keep one on a shelf somewhere in your house. Keep magnets away from computers, computerized cash registers, or other electronic appliances and credit cards. String is harmless, so use that in such cases.

 A SPELL FOR MONEY LUCK

This is a lovely spell that will enhance your cash flow and help you when things are tight. Bless, anoint, and inscribe your name and the words "money luck" onto a green candle. Inscribe the approximate amount of money you need. If you are not sure exactly how much you require, just inscribe "to obtain money."

Place the candle in the center of your pentagram and light it. Place some paper money on the altar. If you can't even come up with that, put your checkbook, savings book, or anything else that represents money onto the altar.

- If you possess a Tarot deck, take out the Ace of Pentacles, the Sun, and the Wheel of Fortune. Spread them out around the candle. Don't rush out and buy a pack of cards if you haven't any; you can get away with writing the names of these cards onto pretty pieces of card or paper and using them instead.

- Make a start on this spell on a Wednesday, on any phase of the moon other than the dark of the moon.

- Do it every day for nine days, using a new, blessed, anointed, and inscribed candle each day.

- Light the candle and recite your prayer of protection for that day, then speak the following:

> *O, angel of luck and money, I direct my plea,*
>
> *The money I need is for the good,*
>
> *And not for the greed.*

[Say this seven times, then say:]

> *So mote it be.*

[Then allow the candle to burn down and out.]

ANOTHER MONEY LUCK SPELL

This spell is similar to the previous money one, but you will need five identical green candles. This particular spell doesn't need to be performed more than once, as it is quite powerful, and usually you should see a result within three days.

- Place the candles in holders, and put one candle on each point of the pentagram.

- Underneath each candle, place a small coin.

- Put your money and Tarot cards on the altar as before.

- If you have designed a wealth amulet, place this on the altar as well.

- Light each candle and visualize a purple pentagram hovering above your own; imagine that you are engulfed in a beautiful white light; and envisage golden coins showering from the visualized pentagram.

Now with sincerity and feeling, take three long deep breaths, and say the following:

I ask the gods and goddesses of the universe

To look upon my need this day.

I have no greed in my heart when I ask for this money.

My need is genuine; my need is great.

The purpose of my request is [say what the money is needed for]

And not for any other need.

Shine thy light of good fortune toward myself

And all those with whom I will bless with your gifts.

So mote it be.

❧

Meditate on the vision for a while and leave all five candles to burn down and out without disturbing them.

AND . . .

This is something that I learned when times were hard, and although it is not strictly magic, it has a similar effect.

Don't allow anybody to *sell* you anything, but take control and only buy what you decide to buy. This means taking every piece of junk mail that comes into the house and throwing it away unopened, because there is nothing in those envelopes that you need, and looking at them will only make you want what you can't afford to have. Also, put a notice outside your house to the effect that you don't want hawkers and sales people coming to your door.

Ignore all advertising on the radio, television, and in the press. Take a totally proactive role by seeking out only those things that you need to buy. This may sound silly, but it allows you to take control of your spending rather than allowing yourself to be seduced by clever sales ploys. Let these clever sales people work their "magic" on those who can afford to be foolish—stay above it all, and choose only what you want to buy.

Work, Business, and Careers

The following spells can improve your working situation. The "I desire" spell can also aid difficult situations at work and can be used alongside these spells.

 A SPELL TO IMPROVE YOUR SUCCESS AT WORK

Day:	Begin on a Sunday
Moon phase:	Waxing
Candle color:	Yellow

This is a nine-day ritual. You will need nine identical yellow candles, using a new one each day.

- Try to conduct this ritual at the same time each day.

- Bless and inscribe the candle with the words "Success at work."

- Anoint a candle, and place it in the center of your pentagram.

- Light the candle.

- Say your protection prayer for Sunday, then recite the following:

> *I ask thee, Archangel Michael, ruler of the sun,*
>
> *To assist me in my magical workings.*
>
> *Give me the confidence and power to show others my abilities.*

Let me shine within my workforce and grow more
successful with each day.

[Recite this three times, then say:]

So mote it be.

✑

[Let the candle burn down and go out.]

 A SPELL TO MAKE A DEMANDING BOSS GENTLE

Day:	Begin on a Saturday
Moon phase:	Full
Candle color:	White

This is a nine-day ritual, but the results are usually immediate. Conduct your spell with good intentions, and guard against directing any dislike or negativity toward the boss.

• Bless and inscribe the candle with the full name of your boss. Then add "to reduce aggression."

• Anoint the candle.

• Take your tools to your radio or television, or any appliance that you can leave on.

• Say your protection prayer for Saturday.

• Place the candle in the center of your pentagram, and recite the following:

I summon thee Archangel Cassiel, ruler of Saturn,

To bring peace into the heart of [person's name].

Make him/her popular with all around him/her.

Let him/her be free of aggression.

[Recite this seven times, then say:]

So mote it be.

[Allow the candle to burn down and go out.]

 A SPELL TO ENJOY YOUR WORK

Day:	Any day of the week
Moon phase:	New
Candle color:	Yellow or gold

This ritual should be conducted every day until you see an improvement.

- Bless and inscribe the candle with the words "[name] to enjoy my work more."

- Anoint the candle, and place it in the center of your pentagram.

- Light the candle and say your protection prayer for whatever day of the week it is.

- Recite the following only once:

I invoke the energies of the cosmos to direct magic my way.

I ask for you to ease the stress of my work and make it more enjoyable.

Bring harmony to my days and success with all I do.

So mote it be.

[Let the candle burn down and out.]

 A SPELL TO IMPROVE CONDITIONS AT WORK

Day: Begin on a Thursday
Moon phase: Any
Candle color: Purple

This spell will help to make the working environment more settled and easier to cope with.

- Prepare and inscribe the candle with your name and the name of the company you work for, followed by the words, "Improve working conditions."

- Place the candle in the center of your pentagram and light it, reciting the following invocation:

Archangel Sachiel, I invoke thee
To aid my magic this day.

Bring light to my place of work.

Let no man hinder or thwart me.

[Recite the spell nine times, then finish with the words:]

So mote it be.

❧

Repeat the spell on five successive days, each time allowing the candle to burn all the way down and out.

 A SPELL TO GET A NEW JOB

Day:	Begin on a Sunday
Moon phase:	New
Candle color:	Yellow
Also:	A small piece of paper

This is a five-day ritual.

- Prepare and inscribe the candle with the words, "To obtain a new job."

- Take the piece of paper and write "new job" on it nine times.

- Light the candle and recite the following:

I summon thee, Archangel Michael, to witness the magic I make.

Bring your power to me and direct your energy into my life.

New work has begun,

From the power of the sun.

[Say this invocation seven times, then say:]

So mote it be.

Allow the candle to burn down and out, then take your piece of paper and mail it to yourself. Repeat the procedure for five days using the methods above, letting the candle burn down and out on each occasion.

 A SPELL TO RECEIVE A PROMOTION

Day: Begin on a Sunday
Moon phase: New
Candle color: Yellow

This spell is a five-day ritual and is best performed in the evenings, starting on the first day of a new moon.

* Prepare and inscribe your name on the candle, along with the word "Promotion."

* Recite the following:

I invoke the powers of universal magic to
Bring forth progression.
I will be recognized for my talent,
I will be chosen.

[After seven recitations, say:]

So mote it be.

Let the candle burn down and out. You will need to repeat this spell on five successive nights.

   A SPELL FOR SUCCESS IN BUSINESS

Day: **Begin on a Thursday**
Moon phase: **Any**
Candle color: **Purple**

Repeat this spell on each of five days.

- Inscribe the candle with the name of the business and the word "Success."

- Put the candle in a holder, place it in the center of your pentagram, and recite the following:

Archangel Sachiel, ruler of Jupiter,

I invoke thee to send forth your magical influence

And bring strength to this failing business.

Let it shine with radiance and good fortune.

With the element of fire, aid this plea.

[Recite the invocation seven times, then say:]

So mote it be.

Be sure to keep a small magnet or a piece of string in your cash register or wallet at all times, as this will attract the money energy that you require. However, these days you must guard against keeping a magnet near any credit cards, as it will wipe the information that is contained in them.

 A SPELL TO BECOME BETTER AT YOUR JOB

Day: Begin on a Thursday
Moon phase: Waxing
Candle color: Purple

This is a five-day ritual.

* Inscribe the candle with your name and the words "Success at work."

* Put the candle in a holder and recite the following:

Archangel Raphael, ruler of Mercury,

I invoke thee to send forth your element of air

And to shine down your magical influence.

Bring strength to my abilities and

Let me shine with radiance.

[Recite the invocation seven times, then say:]

So mote it be.

Repeat this for five days as above, allowing each candle to burn down and out.

 A SPELL FOR LUCK WITH GAMBLING

Day: Begin on a Thursday
Moon phase: Full or waxing
Candle color: Green or purple

Should you wish to try your luck on the lottery or to back a horse, perform the following spell. This is a nine-day ritual that must be performed at the same time each day. Good luck!

• Place on the altar a lottery ticket, football coupon, betting slip, or whatever item is related to your gambling effort.

• Also place a checkbook or money in paper form next to it.

• If you have a Tarot deck, take out the Ace of Pentacles and the Ace of Cups, and place these around the pentagram. If you don't own a Tarot deck, write the names of these cards on two pretty pieces of paper and use those instead.

• Bless and inscribe the candle with the word "winner" and the amount you wish to win.

• Anoint the candle and light it.

• Say your protection prayer for Thursday.

- Recite the following:

O, angel of luck and fortune, shower me with your grace.

Bring forth the power to assist me and make me win this day.

[Recite this five times, then say:]

So mote it be.

Then let the candle burn down and out. Repeat this for nine straight days.

Don't always expect your win to come in the way you imagine. You may win a raffle or a contest. Always remember that when you do win, give a little away; it needn't be much, but a token gesture is always appropriate.

15

Love Spells

We all long for the ideal lover who will share our thoughts and feelings and who can understand and support us in everything that we do. We know that nature intends men and women to join forces for obvious reasons such as procreation, but most of us spend our entire lives seeking our soul mate. While some of us are fortunate enough to find the perfect partner, many seem destined not to do so.

Those who give readings to the public, whether they have trained in the Wiccan tradition or come to it in any other way, soon discover that the client who has a problem in his or her love life will be extremely anxious and upset. They are frequently far more wound up than those who have more important things on their minds. I think that the main reason for this is that, unlike love, people feel able to exert some control over matters such as money, work, living conditions, and so on.

Health problems are as intractable as those of love, but people understand that these are in the hands of the gods, the universe, or fate, rather than down to someone else's obstinate refusal (as they see it) to give them what they long for. It is tempting to think that magic and spells will change the other person's heart, but this is a dangerous road to go down, as we shall soon see. The only spell that affects the actions of another person that is worth performing is the one that takes the other person away and out of one's life.

Spiritual teachings suggest that spirit does not allow us to reincarnate with our soul mates, because we would become so wrapped up in them that we would cease to learn. We learn something from every relationship, so each one is important to our spiritual development. Love spells work, but this is an area where caution is needed; it can be dangerous to influence the minds of others through rituals, and it is not really accepted practice among witches. Witches believe that we end up where we are meant to be, but we also understand that although we follow the destiny that the spirit world maps out for us, we are also free to exercise choice where affairs of the heart are concerned.

Over the centuries, men have tended to call their attractive, young mistresses temptresses, and some have even complained that they were bewitched into their affairs. Perhaps this relieved their guilt . . . but who knows? Some steamy love affairs may even have been brought into being by one or two pink candles and a few hot invocations.

I have always been a great believer in love spells, although I have had a few hiccups with them in the past. Any experienced witch will tell you that some rituals for love can be dangerous, as these are the most powerful spells of all—and if they are not conducted carefully, they can cause chaos. I can feel myself sighing as I

Practical Spellcraft

write this, because I know that you will ignore this good advice—I know that in my turn, I ignored it, too.

But still, at the risk of being a killjoy, I must warn you of the dangers of playing with magic where love is concerned. These spells are very easy to cast, and a simple "I desire" type of spell can be extremely difficult to undo. By performing such a spell, we tap into the subconscious mind of the other person, and only a very strong individual can resist the effects of a love spell. Believe it or not, it isn't just women who cast spells for love; men are as much to blame. Here are some illuminating stories for you . . .

Examples

SUSAN AND BRIAN

Susan meets Brian; he thinks she's nice enough, but Susan is really smitten by Brian. He doesn't really pursue her, so his cool attitude stirs all kinds of strange emotions, and Susan soon finds herself thinking about him day and night.

At last, Susan decides to cast a spell to win his affection. Brian responds and becomes more attracted to her, and Susan enjoys this affection for six whole months. Then along comes another nice chap, and she begins to tire of Brian. Brian is devastated, and he never gets over Susan.

TERRY AND LIZ

Terry is attracted to Liz, but Liz is married to a nice man—and has been for ten years. Terry aches to seduce Liz, so he performs a spell to win her over.

134

Terry and Liz begin the affair. Liz leaves her husband to be with Terry, but she brings her five children with her. A year down the line, Terry has had enough of Liz's children and also her constant nagging, so he comes to regret his magical pursuit of Liz.

JANET AND PETER

Janet is attracted to Peter, but he doesn't even know that Janet exists. Janet decides to cast a spell, but Peter is a strong person who knows his own mind. He becomes aware of Janet, but he is also aware that there is absolutely nothing he likes about her.

The spell then bounces off him and lands back with Janet. She now becomes so obsessed and besotted with Peter that she never recovers from the experience.

A Cautionary Tale

A fellow witch friend of mine was spending a lot of time with a male friend. During the space of a few months, she discovered that she really liked him and that she wanted things to go further. He was quite content with her friendship; he enjoyed debating with her, and he respected her opinions and ideas, but he had no desire to take things further.

My friend tried all of the usual methods, such as flirting, having cozy chats over coffee, and "accidentally" falling over the cat and landing on his knee. However, she came to the sad conclusion that she could probably swing stark naked from a chandelier, and he wouldn't even notice.

When her infatuation reached boiling point, she dug out a battered old spell book that had been passed down to her by her

mother. The spell that she chose to perform was very ancient—
and here's where the story takes a nasty turn and becomes a dangerous tale. She made a wax effigy resembling the man, and taking a small pin, she tenderly pushed it into the heart of the effigy to symbolize that his heart would be forever open to her. She then melted the effigy in a saucepan and buried it in the garden, supposedly to make his heart melt for her and to invoke love in his heart until the day he died.

Somehow, it didn't quite work out that way. A few days after she had performed her spell, the man contacted her in a panicky state, saying that he had a nagging pain in his chest. His doctor referred him to a specialist, who ran some tests and discovered that he had acquired a heart condition. This was very strange, because the man was only thirty-six years of age. He is still alive today only because this witch's wise mother ran extensive spell-reversals—part of which consisted of digging up the wax image from the garden. Fortunately, the man's condition hasn't deteriorated.

This story is absolutely true—and even writing this piece still makes me wince. So, student witches, even when you have been practicing spellcasting for many years, don't delve too deeply into this subject. Keep it light-hearted, and please bear in mind that you might end up doing more harm than good.

On the Other Hand...

A far happier tale is the way that I met my partner, which was through a love spell—although this happened by accident!

One day, one of my students telephoned me and told me that she was feeling down in the dumps, as she had been looking for

Love Spells

Mr. Right for quite a while. So she asked me to give her a harmless love spell to try. I agreed to this, and I began to recite the spell over the telephone. It was quite a long spell, and I must have been on the phone for over an hour while she wrote down every word that I said. The end portion of the spell read, "This must be performed on a Friday at the time of the full moon and a pink candle must be lit in the process."

The student and I soon found ourselves giggling, as it was a Friday, and we were in a full moon phase. I suggested that she should perform the spell immediately. We cut the connection, and I got on with my work. About an hour later, I noticed that among the candles that I had been burning that evening, there, as proud as punch, stood a tall, elegant, candy-pink candle. The thought crossed my mind that while reciting the spell to my student, I had actually said the invocation myself. Not thinking anymore of it, I went about my business. Three days later, I met the love of my life! We have been together ever since, and we are extremely happy.

The spells that I have included in this book are tried and tested and safe to use. However, there are sometimes specific circumstances that one cannot foresee, so be sure to use a good dollop of common sense in whatever you do. I have listed some necessary advice and warnings, so please take this part of the book seriously and be very careful.

Warnings

- Never conduct a love spell without fully assessing the situation first.

- Never cast a spell if you think that the other person isn't likely to become really interested. There should be clear, mutual benefit—not just for one person.

- Never cast a spell for someone who is attached to someone else.

- Think very carefully before casting the spell, because it may not be what you want in the long run.

- It is best not to cast a spell on behalf of another person, because the person that they want could easily fall for you instead!

- Never conduct a love spell with which you are unfamiliar.

- Never perform a spell for eternal love for someone— even if you are married to the person.

- Always take the potency of love spells very seriously.

- Never conduct love spells for fun.

- And *never* cast a spell from old, battered, ancient books that consist of pin sticking, wax melting, and burials!

Advice

- You can cast a spell for a wonderful lover.

- You can cast a spell for someone if you are pretty sure that your feelings will be returned.

- You can give a person a gentle push in the right direction.

- You can cast a spell for a person to gain the confidence to ask you out.

- You can cast a spell to appear more attractive to the one you desire.

- You can do a "notice me" spell.

- You can cast a spell for a little more passion in your life.

- You can cast a spell to attract the attention of a lover if you are single, but this isn't recommended if you're married, because the spell could rebound, and your partner could be the one to have an affair.

- You can cast a spell so that the one you want will be at the right place at the right time.

- Oh, and yes. You *are* allowed to fall in love! That's not against the rules.

- Enjoy your spellcasting—but do take care!

A SPELL TO MAKE YOURSELF IRRESISTIBLE

Day: Begin on a Friday
Moon phase: Full
Candle color: Pink

- Inscribe the candle with your name and the word "irresistible."

- Anoint the candle with oil.

- Place the best photo of yourself you can find on the altar, along with a lock of your hair and a piece of white ribbon.

- Say your protection prayer for Friday.

- Recite the following:

I have the desire to be irresistible to the opposite sex,

No person will dismiss me.

My charms are enticing to this I'm inviting.

[Once you have said this three times, say:]

So mote it be.

On the evening that you cast this spell, gather together a small handkerchief or towel, a red button, and your favorite scent. Place the button in the handkerchief, along with a rough drawing of this person, inscribed with his or her name. Fold all four corners together and tie it with a red ribbon. Finally, spray it with your chosen scent and wear the same perfume that night. Carry the spell around with you on your person.

A SPELL TO BE NOTICED BY THE ONE YOU DESIRE

Warning! Do not perform this spell if the person you fancy is attached to another.

Day: Begin on a Friday
Moon phase: Full
Candle color: Red (for intensity)

- Bless the candle.

- Inscribe your name and add, "to be noticed by [name the one you desire]."

- Anoint the candle.

- Place it on the altar in the center of your pentagram.

- Light the candle, and recite the following:

Archangel Anael,

I seek your assistance in bringing the power you possess,

To make [name of desired] see me and no other.

Let [his or her] heart be warm in my presence.

As the flame burns, let [his or her] desire flow to me.

And So mote it be.

[As usual, let the candle burn down and out.]

A SPELL TO ATTRACT LOVE

Day: **Begin on a Friday**
Moon phase: Full
Candle color: Pink

- With a small knife, inscribe your name on the candle and the words, "To attract love."

- Choose a quiet corner of your house (not necessarily your altar); place the candle in the center of your pentagram.

- If you know who it is that you want to attract, place a photo of the person in front of the candle.

- Take a piece of red ribbon and wrap it around your left hand three times. Sit facing your candle.

- If you have a deck of Tarot cards, place the Lovers, the Two of Cups, and the High Priestess on the altar. If you do not, then write the names of these cards on some pretty pieces of paper and use those instead.

- Recite the following:

Archangel Anael,

I require your assistance to bring power with love.

I summon thee to bring love to my being together in harmony and peace.

Let the light shine strength and force upon me.

[Recite the spell three times, then say:]

So mote it be.

[Repeat this spell each day for the next five days.]

 A SPELL TO EASE THE LOSS OF LOVE

Day: Begin on a Friday
Moon phase: Waxing
Candle color: Yellow

This is a nine-day ritual.

- Bless the candle, and inscribe your name and "To ease the loss of love."

- Anoint the candle, and place it in the center of your pentagram.

- The following is to be recited nine times on each day:

Archangel Anael,
I require strength from the cosmos
To ease the loss of love within my heart.
It is not the wish of the Angels for myself and [name]
To be to be joined in unity for eternity,
So envelop me with the courage and power to move forward.

The spell is made.

[After the ninth recitation, say:]

So mote it be.

[Allow the candle to burn down and out.]

 ## A SPELL TO SAVE A MARRIAGE

Day: Begin on a Friday
Moon phase: New
Candle color: Pink

Inscribe both your name and the name of your partner on a prepared candle.

- Place the candle in the center of the pentagram.

- On the five points of the star, place five white, blessed, and anointed candles.

- Place some flowers on the altar. These can be any type or variety.

- Next, place a wedding photograph or a photo of both of you.

- Take both wedding rings and tie them together with a red ribbon. This may be a problem, but you could try telling your spouse that you are taking the rings to be cleaned and polished. Failing this, find some other piece of jewelry that belongs to your spouse.

- Put the rings on the altar.

- Light the candle and say your protection prayer for the day.

- Recite the following once, then allow the candles to burn down and extinguish themselves. Do not disturb the altar once the spell is in operation.

Archangel Anael, great god of love,

Bring the power forth to repair this marriage.

Bring sweetness back to this unity and

Fill it with serenity.

With the binding of these rings,

I ask you to restore completeness

And bring us together as one again.

Let your power be directed to this magic.

So mote it be.

 A SPELL TO REINVIGORATE A RELATIONSHIP

If your relationship has become a little flat, and you would like to spice it up a bit—this should have an immediate effect. This is a three-day ritual.

Day:	**Begin on a Friday**
Moon phase:	**Full**
Candle color:	**Red**

Prepare a red candle by blessing and anointing it, and inscribe the names of both yourself and your partner.

- Also inscribe the words, "Revitalize relationship."

- Place your candle in the center of the pentagram, and say your Friday prayer.

- Light the candle and recite the following:

Bring life to this unity.

Bring passion and rebirth.

Intensify the feelings we once shared.

Let the flames of desire burn like the flame from this candle.

[Recite this nine times, then say:]

So mote it be.

Perform this ritual for three days, altering your protection prayer each day to make it appropriate for the day. Now allow the candle to extinguish itself.

 A SPELL TO REMOVE SOMEONE FROM YOUR MIND

There are times when we become obsessed or infatuated with another person, and this can really hinder our lives, especially when we know in our hearts that we are barking up the wrong tree.

This spell will banish all thoughts of the person and leave you free to get on with your life. This is a nine-day ritual.

Day: **Begin on a Tuesday**
Moon phase: **Waning**
Candle color: **White**

- Prepare a white candle by blessing and anointing it, then inscribe your name on the candle.

- Next inscribe the name of the one you wish to banish from your thoughts; once you have done this, draw a line through the center of their name.

- Place the candle in the center of your pentagram, and say your prayer of protection for Tuesday.

- Visualize yourself walking away from the person.

- Now recite the following:

I hereby banish all thoughts from my mind,

My wishes are pure, my feelings are kind.

Bring freedom to me from the one I desire.

[Recite this nine times, then say:]

So mote it be.

Allow the candle to burn down and out. Repeat the ritual for the next eight days.

A SPELL TO IMPROVE A RELATIONSHIP

Day: Begin on a Friday
Moon phase: New
Candle color: White

- Bless and inscribe the candle with the words, "To improve the relationship of [name] and [name]."

- Anoint the candle, and place it in the center of your pentagram.

- Place a photograph of yourself and your lover on the altar.

- Try to acquire a lock of your lover's hair, and place this on the altar.

- Take a piece of red ribbon, and wrap it around your left hand three times.

- Sit facing your altar.

- If you have a deck of Tarot cards, place the Lovers, the Two of Cups, and the High Priestess on the altar. If you do not, then write the name of these three cards on pretty pieces of paper and use them instead.

- Recite the following:

Archangel Anael,

I require your assistance to bring power with love.

I summon thee to bring [name] and [name] together in harmony and peace.

Let there no longer be discord,

Shine strength and force upon us.

[Recite the spell three times, then say:]

So mote it be.

Do this spell every day until you see an improvement. It works quickly unless your relationship has run its course, and the spirit world has other plans for you.

 A SPELL TO REMOVE AN OBSESSION

This is best done on a waning moon and on a Thursday. For this spell use a small thin candle of a color that links with the sign of the zodiac of the person whom you want out of your life.

Sign	Color
Aries	Red
Taurus	Pink
Gemini	Yellow
Cancer	White
Leo	Gold or orange
Virgo	Beige or a misty mauve
Libra	Green
Scorpio	Magenta
Sagittarius	Royal blue
Capricorn	Brown or grey
Aquarius	Any neon color
Pisces	Sea-blue or sea-green

- Take a small piece of paper in a color that matches the person's sun sign.

- Take a tiny piece of something that the person has given you. Ensure that this is something that can be destroyed by fire.

- Put the candle, the paper, and the piece of material on a saucer on your drain board or in your sink—preferably facing south, if that is possible.

- Ask for the person to be safely sent out of your life. It is actually a good idea to ask for the person to travel away somewhere safe.

- Allow the candle to burn down, but before it has extinguished itself, burn the paper and the piece of material or object that belonged to the other person.

- Once the candle has extinguished itself, gather up all the remaining ashes and put them into a small paper or plastic bag.

- Take the remains to a stream and throw them in. Watch them float downstream while mentally saying goodbye and wishing the other person well.

 A SPELL TO BRING PASSION INTO YOUR LIFE

Day: Begin on a Tuesday
Moon phase: New or full
Candle color: Red

- Bless and inscribe the candle with your name or the name of the person you are helping.

- Anoint the candle, and place in the center of your pentagram.

- Place a small bowl of sand on the altar.

- Say your protection prayer for Tuesday, and recite the following:

I summon thee, Archangel Samuel, ruler of the planets,

To arouse the passion of [name]

And to make me become too hard for him/her to resist.

[Recite this five times, then say:]

So mote it be.

Perform this spell every night until the chosen partner's sex drive returns.

 A SPELL TO CONTACT THE PERSON YOU DESIRE

This spell can be performed on any day of the week and during any moon phase, because it works by the power of thought.

If you have had no contact with someone and wish to see the person, go to bed just before midnight. Lie flat on your back and meditate for a few minutes, clearing your mind of all the day's events, then concentrate hard on the person that you wish to contact. Imagine them walking toward you, and imagine yourself talking to them. If it is love that you want, imagine the two of you making love.

Continue with this meditation for two or three more minutes. Next, hold out your hands and imagine that you are holding a glass ball. Cup your hands around the imaginary ball. Take about one minute to do this. Feel the ball within your hands getting hotter, then imagine that it is getting cooler, until it becomes icy cold.

Raise your hands above your head (still holding on to the ball) for a few moments, bring back the thought of the person you want to contact, then throw the ball into the universe. Your thoughts will have been transmitted into the imaginary ball and will now be sent to the other person.

This spell should need to be performed only once, but it may take some practice, so continue with it every night until you have mastered the art of telepathy.

 A SPELL TO HEAL A RIFT BETWEEN LOVERS

This spell is useful for those times when you quarrel with your lover or when your relationship is flagging, and you need to bring something good back into it.

This spell can be performed on any day of the week and during any moon phase, but a waxing or waning moon is preferable. It is best to do this spell during the evening, when your home is quiet.

- Buy two tall, tapered, pink candles.
- Bless the candles in the usual way.

- At the top of the candles (near the wick), inscribe one with your name and the other with your partner's name, but try not to make the lettering too big.

- Run yourself a bath and place the candles in the bathroom as near to the bath as possible.

- Turn off your main lights and bathe by candlelight. (Very relaxing!)

- Next, add two teaspoons of salt to your bath and a few drops of rosemary oil.

- Relax in the bath and meditate on the lit candles.

- As the flames start to melt the names of your partner and yourself, imagine that the fire is destroying any discord between you.

- Try to stay in the bath for half an hour or so, continuing with the meditation.

- Extinguish the flames, ensuring that the wax has melted both names, but don't get out of the bath until the inscriptions have gone.

You should find that your relationship starts to improve, or the personality of your partner starts to soften.

16

Spells for Fertility and Children

Children are born with a natural inclination toward spiritual matters, and they are closer to the spirit world than we are, so you may have heard stories of children who have had imaginary friends or have had strange experiences. This is quite normal, to the point that some teachings suggest that guides closely protect children, and some children are so perceptive that they sometimes see their guides or communicate with them.

When my children ask questions on the subject of magic, I always answer them honestly. They are not old enough to be really aware of my beliefs, but my eldest child collects crystals, and he regularly meditates with them.

If you have children, it is quite acceptable to perform rituals for their well-being. The following spells may be performed as and when necessary.

A SPELL TO AID CONCEPTION

Day: Begin on a Monday
Moon phase: Full
Candle color: White, silver, pale blue, or green

Perform this ritual once on the night of every full moon until the woman in question becomes pregnant.

- Bless and inscribe the candle with the name of the person who wishes to become pregnant and the words, "To become pregnant."

- Anoint the candle, and place it in the center of your pentagram.

- For the best results, this spell should be performed as late in the evening as possible; however, as you shouldn't leave your candle unattended overnight, if you need to get to bed early, it would be better to perform it in the early evening.

- Take a lock of the woman's hair and place it on the altar in front of the candle.

- Visualize the woman being pregnant and glowing with health. Then envisage her in labor and holding her child afterward.

- Say your protection prayer for Monday.

- Recite the following, and as you speak, take a length (a meter or a yard) of white baby ribbon and wind it around your hand until it runs out.

Archangel Gabriel,

I summon and conjure thee this day to radiate the powers

Of the moon toward [name].

Let the barren womb be planted with the seed of life,

And bring a healthy child to her.

[Recite the spell twice, then say:]

So mote it be.

❧

[Allow the candle to burn down and out.]

(NOTE: You could also design a fertility amulet for the woman to keep thereafter.)

Spells for Children

All the following spells should be begun on a Monday, under any phase of the moon. The candles should be white. The invocations should be recited nine times and conducted every day until you see an improvement.

You must bless and inscribe the child's full name on the candle, along with the title of the spell. Anoint the candle, and place it in the center of your pentagram. Say your protection prayer for Monday (and for each subsequent day thereafter), and for a few minutes prior to reciting the spell, try to visualize the child achieving the desired outcome. **Follow the spells word for word; do not adapt them in any way.**

A SPELL TO CALM A CRYING BABY

Inscribe "To stop crying" on the candle, and recite the following:

Bring peace to the heart of this divine child,

Calm the spirit within,

May harmonious rays shine down to his/her soul.

Let the quiet begin.

The spell is made,

And So mote it be.

[Now allow the candle to burn down and out.]

 A SPELL TO HELP A CHILD SLEEP THROUGH THE NIGHT

Inscribe "To sleep through the night" on the candle, and recite:

O, heavenly Mother Earth, hear my plea,

Bring sleep unto this child for me.

Make his/her rest be still and peaceful through the night.

And So mote it be.

[Now allow the candle to burn down and out.]

A SPELL TO SWEETEN A CHILD'S MOOD

Inscribe "To sweeten [child's name]'s mood," and recite:

Angel Gabriel, ruler of the moon,

Shower this child with the influence you possess.

Make his/her temperament calm.

Bring forth sweetness to his/her nature.

And So mote it be.

[Now allow the candle to burn down and out.]

 A SPELL TO PROTECT A CHILD FROM MISFORTUNE

Inscribe "To protect [child's name] from life's misfortunes," and recite:

O, archangels of the universe,

Bring good to [name] in all he/she does.

Protect him/her from all of the evil

That the earth breeds, and lead him/her to the light.

And So mote it be.

[Now let the candle burn down and out.]

A SPELL TO STOP SIBLING RIVALRY AND FIGHTING

Inscribe "To bring peace into the hearts of [name] and [name]," and recite:

I call upon the Archangel Raphael,

To intervene and cease the anger

Between [name] and [name].

Bring their souls together united and aid their

Spiritual development.

And So mote it be.

[Now allow the candle to burn down and out.]

 A SPELL TO IMPROVE A CHILD'S CONCENTRATION

Inscribe "To improve the concentration of [name]," and recite:

I cast my magic to summon the Archangel Raphael,

To aid the concentration of [name].

Let him/her shine in thy light.

And So mote it be.

[Now allow the candle to burn down and out.]

A SPELL TO ENHANCE A CHILD'S ACADEMIC ABILITY

Inscribe the child's name and "To improve academic ability," and recite:

Angel of wisdom, assist me this day,

Let [name] be free from distraction, and grow with

Extreme intelligence.

And So mote it be.

[Now let the candle burn down and out.]

 A SPELL TO MAKE A CHILD MORE CONFIDENT

Inscribe the child's name and "To be more confident," and recite:

Let this child I love,

Show light and attraction to all he/she meets.

Fill his/her being with confidence.

Bring popularity in abundance.

And So mote it be.

[Now let the candle burn down and out.]

A SPELL TO PREVENT A CHILD FROM BEING A BULLY

Inscribe the child's name and "To prevent from being a bully," and recite:

> *O, Angel of Mercy, I call upon you this day,*
>
> *To bring tranquillity into the heart of [name].*
>
> *Let him/her be discouraged from violence;*
>
> *Let peace be in his/her heart forever.*
>
> *And So mote it be.*

[Now let the candle burn down and out.]

 A SPELL TO PROTECT A CHILD FROM A BULLY

Inscribe the child's name and "To prevent from being bullied," and recite:

> *Let no soul torment,*
>
> *Let no soul injure.*
>
> *Deliver a tranquil existence into the life of [name].*
>
> *Let the enemies he/she possesses be hindered in their attempts.*
>
> *Bring peace into the hearts of them.*
>
> *So mote it be.*

[Now let the candle burn down and out.]

A SPELL TO BANISH A BAD INFLUENCE

Inscribe the name of the person whose influence you wish to dispel and the word "Banish," and recite:

Archangel Raphael,

I need your assistance in ridding the influence of [name]

From my child [name]'s life.

I wish no misfortune upon this person,

Only to leave my child in peace.

Let your powers be strong in working this magic.

And So mote it be.

[Now let the candle burn down and out.]

A SPELL TO HEAL A CHILD WHO IS SICK

Inscribe the name of child and "To aid recovery," and recite:

I summon all of the archangels of the cosmos to help

In the magical practice I perform this day.

Shower [name] with your healing energy,

And direct him/her into good, everlasting health.

Radiate healing light around him/her.

Bring protection to his/her being.

And So mote it be.

[Now let the candle burn down and out.]

17

Animal Magic

Most witches have an affinity with animals and surround themselves with many different kinds of them. Of course, the cat is identified with being the familiar, but a variety of creatures will happily live alongside her. Witches believe that animals are as important as people are and that our pets are known to be the spokesmen of the animal kingdom. Without them, we wouldn't learn to understand the importance of creatures or even begin to realize their role in life.

We are lucky because we have a voice; animals rely on us for their care. In return, they give us a very precious gift, one that our human companions often find very difficult to share—their love.

They say that when you love an animal, you are in tune with the earth and all that resides on it. Special people love animals. To understand a person is easy, but to understand an animal is not so easy. Half the time, you have to put up with antisocial behavior: a dog that chews your couch or a cat that drinks from your toilet bowl or fights with every other cat in the neighborhood. These animals are important to the evolution of our souls, and they captivate most of us at some time in our lives.

We live alongside animals, and we share their space. We eat them to live—and in some situations, they would do the same thing to us—but we must also respect a creature that has a more defined knowledge of nature than we have. Wild animals know when the weather is going to change, they sense danger more quickly than we do, and many have a maternal side that is as strong as that of any human mother.

We are so fortunate to live in these times, for we have been given the opportunity to experience not only the animals we surround ourselves with on a daily basis but also the more distant and exotic ones that we see on the television. This helps us to understand how the world works.

Spells for Animals

Here are a couple of spells that you may wish to use for your pets at some time or another.

 A SPELL TO HELP A SICK OR INJURED ANIMAL

Day:	Begin on any day
Moon phase:	Any
Candle color:	White

• Bless and inscribe your candle with the name of your pet and the words "Good health."

- Anoint the candle in the usual way, and place it in the center of your pentagram.

- Say your protection prayer for the day, and recite the following:

O, Lord and master, take pity on this creature before you.

Send forth healing power,

And restore him/her to strength.

Vitality is the answer.

[Say this nine times, then say:]

So mote it be.

]Allow the candle to burn down and go out.]

 A SPELL TO FIND A LOST PET

I conducted this spell only last year, when my beloved cat, Nino, disappeared. After the first couple of days, I began to panic, because he wasn't the type to wander far. After ten days' absence, this spell brought him back. He was a little thin and dehydrated, but safe and well.

- On the pentagram atop your prepared altar, bless and anoint five white candles.

- Place one on each point of the star.

- Next, prepare a yellow candle, inscribing the pet's name on it.

- Place this in the center of your pentagram.

- From your garden, take a petal from every flower, and scatter them on the altar.

- If your pet has certain toys or playthings, place these on the altar also.

- Light all of the candles, and repeat the following invocation once:

I speak these words from my heart in the hope

That the great god of all creatures living

Will aid me in my magical work.

Send guidance to [name of pet] and return him/her

To the safety of his/her home.

Let no harm fall upon him/her.

Send forth this message with haste.

And So mote it be.

Witches "Familiars"

We are all accustomed to the image of a witch riding her broomstick, her faithful black cat sitting in front of her. In days gone by, people thought that all witches kept some small animal, such as a frog, as a "familiar." It was believed that the witch fed her familiar with milk from her own body—despite the fact that some witches were men! It was also believed that the witch would send her familiar out to do harm to others.

These days, we know that witches make their spells to help people, and they use their knowledge of herbs to heal people. Many also perform their rituals to heal the earth. We know that the last thing that any bona fide witch would want is to bring harm to any person. We also know that their pets are just pets and nothing more. But is this really so?

If you decide to visit a person who is elderly, sick, or down at heart (and especially a sick child), and if you have the kind of pet that you can take along with you, try doing so. You will find that your pet will bring a smile to your sick friend's face, and it will lift his or her spirits. This means, in essence, that your pet *does* have the power to heal, and that it is truly a valuable familiar.

18

Spells for Health

We cannot always intervene in health conditions, because we are given certain health problems as part of our spiritual growth and development. During the course of our many lifetimes, we need to learn about the many human conditions and emotions, so pain and discomfort are ones that assist us in reaching a higher spiritual level.

With each lifetime, we learn many important lessons, each of which makes us wiser and stronger, and each helps us to build our character. It is said that before we reincarnate, we speak with our angels, and they tell us about the lessons that we will learn during the coming life, and these may include health issues.

I may feel sorry to see someone who is in a wheelchair or a person who has had some accident that has left him to suffer disabilities, but I am also aware that this may be the person's karma. However, it is right for us to sympathize with the misfortunes that others suffer, because we could just as easily reincarnate next time into a similar situation.

You may wish to cast a spell to aid someone's recovery, but I have to be honest with you and tell you that while such spells can bring relief, they rarely cure a person of his illness. This becomes even more apparent when it comes to the subject of mental health. I have tried many times to help mentally ill people, and I have come to the realization that it simply doesn't work.

This could be because we are innocently attempting to influence a person's mind, and this is not really allowed in magic. Another possibility is that spirit may have given the person the disability to help others grow by being caretakers for that person. This gives such people as care workers, doctors, and nurses the opportunity to work on their karma, as well. Sick, disabled, and mentally ill people are there for the benefit of so many of us on our evolutionary road.

In view of all this, I will give you a simple general health spell that you can perform if someone is temporarily sick. This will cover everything from headaches through hospitalization, and it may, at least, give the sufferer a little relief. Often, just the good thoughts that are sent out help the person's body fight the sickness and recover. Even if there is nothing more to be gained than giving the sick person the feeling that someone cares enough to do something for him, this can make it worth the effort.

A General Health Spell

Health spells can be performed on any day of the week, although it is preferable to conduct them in the morning.

- Always use a white or yellow candle, blessing and anointing it in the usual way.

- Inscribe the person's name, along with the health problem and the word "Banish."

- Recite the following:

O, archangels of the universe, I ask your assistance this day

To combine your powers together and help [name]
to reach a full recovery.

Let no more suffering bestow on him/her,

Bring peace and health before him/her.

Cast your healing rays in his/her direction.

[Recite this seven times, then say:]

And So mote it be.

[Allow the candle to burn itself out.]

A Prayer for the Departed

If someone you know is near to death, or if they have already left the earth plane, use the following spell—it will help the soul to pass peacefully into the spirit realm.

- Bless and anoint five white candles in the usual way.

- You need not inscribe the candles.

- Place one candle on each point of the pentagram, and light them.

- Recite the following just once:

> *I ask thee, divine spirit, to take [name]*
>
> *From this planet into a peaceful existence.*
>
> *Let the angel protecting him/her carry him/her*
>
> *Safely into your heaven.*
>
> *Bring understanding to those who are left behind*
>
> *And let his/her light of being shine down upon those he/she loved.*
>
> *Let us all be united together someday*
>
> *In the brilliance of your power,*
>
> *And let his/her footsteps on this earth carry importance*
>
> *Forever with your divine force.*
>
> *And So mote it be.*

[Now allow the candles to burn down and out.]

19

An Assortment of Useful Spells

 A SPELL FOR PROTECTION WHEN TRAVELING

Day: Begin on a Wednesday
Moon phase: Any
Candle color: Green or yellow

- Bless and inscribe your candle with the name or names of those who intend to travel and the words, "To be protected on my/our journey."

- Anoint the candle, and place it in the center of your pentagram.

- If you are traveling by air, burn sandalwood incense during this spell, as this spice represents flight and adds intensity to the spell.

- Light the candle, and say your protection prayer for Wednesday.

- Recite the following:

Archangel Raphael, guardian of the planet Mercury,

I summon thee, to assist my magic

And bring protection to me while I travel on my journey.

Take me safely to my/our destination.

[Recite this nine times, then say:]

And So mote it be.

[Then let the candle burn down and out.]

 A SPELL TO IMPROVE CONCENTRATION

This spell needs to be conducted each day for nine days.

Day:	Begin on a Wednesday
Moon phase:	Waning
Candle color:	Yellow (white, as an alternative)

- Bless and inscribe your candle, "To improve concentration," then add your name.

- Anoint the candle in the usual way.

- Place the candle in the center of your pentagram.

- Say your protection prayer for Wednesday.

- Recite the following:

I have the power within my being,

To concentrate on all that's seen.

Raise my awareness, let me be

Alert in thought.

[Recite this nine times, then say:]

So mote it be.

[Then let the candle burn down and out.]

 A SPELL TO BANISH LUSTFUL THOUGHTS

Day:	Begin on a Tuesday
Moon phase:	Waning
Candle color:	White

- Bless and inscribe your candle with the words, "Overcome lust." Add your name or the name of the person for whom you wish to make the spell.

- Anoint the candle and place in the center of your pentagram.

- Now bless five more white candles and anoint them, but do not inscribe them.

- Place these on each of the five points of the pentagram.

- Light all six candles, and say your protection prayer for Tuesday.

- Recite the following:

Purity is within my [or his/her name]'s soul,

Banish corruption.

Lift my [his/her] thoughts to a higher realm.

I [he/she] need(s) not the evil within, but innocence and love.

[Recite this seven times, then say:]

So mote it be.

[Then let the candles burn down and out.]

 A SPELL TO BECOME MORE POPULAR

Conduct this spell on nine consecutive days.

Day:	Begin on a Sunday
Moon phase:	Waxing or new
Candle color:	Yellow

- Bless the candle, and inscribe your name and the words, "Improve popularity."

- Anoint the candle, and place in the center of your pentagram.

- Light the candle.

- Visualize people walking toward you, smiling.

- Say your protection prayer for Sunday.

- Recite the following :

Archangel Michael, I summon thee,

To make me liked by all I see.

I command respect from all I know,

With this, my acceptance will grow.

[Recite this nine times, then say:]

So mote it be.

[Then let the candle burn down and out.]

 A SPELL TO RELIEVE HOPELESSNESS

We are all faced with a hopeless situation at some time in our lives. This spell will give outstanding results and can make you see things more clearly and cope better. The magic works in a way that will bring about your attunement with your angel, who may speak to you through your subconscious while you are asleep or during a meditation. You will certainly have a calmer approach to life and a feeling of well-being after you have conducted the spell.

Day: Any of the week
Moon phase: Any
Candle color: Pale blue or white

You are about to summon your spiritual guide or guardian angel. Every person has a guide that works with him or her through life, and with this spell, you will be asking your guide to move closer to you and help you overcome your problem.

- You only need to bless your candle. It is not necessary to anoint or inscribe it.

- Light the candle, and place it in the center of your pentagram.

- Sit quietly in front of your altar, meditating on the lit candle.

- Close your eyes, and clear your mind.

- Take several deep breaths.

- Try to focus on the darkness behind your closed eyes; you may see lights or images.

- Continue with this until you feel totally relaxed.

- Imagine that you are in a cocoon of light; feel the warmth encircling you.

- Instead of saying this invocation out loud, say it in your mind. Remember that you must mean every word and concentrate on every thought. Keep your eyes closed, and say the following in your head:

O, beautiful angel of mine, please hear my plea today,

My life is distressing, and I require your help to move forward.

I can see no solution to my problems; I can see no way ahead.

Bring your wisdom into my mind, and help me find the answers.

Walk alongside me until I can see my way clearly.

Envelop me in your love forever.

And So mote it be.

Now concentrate on your problem, while imagining how you would like things to be; imagine the perfect situation. Continue sitting and meditating for about fifteen minutes. You can spend longer on this if you wish. Before you leave the spell, open your eyes, and look into the flame of the candle. You may feel quite light-headed after this spell, but that is not unusual.

Many people report that they see their guide during this ritual, or that the problem they were facing suddenly disappears. When you have completed the spell, wait one hour, then blow out the candle, watching the smoke rise upward.

 A SPELL TO IMPROVE MUSICAL TALENT

You need only perform this spell for three days.

Day:	Begin on a Friday
Moon phase:	Waxing
Candle color:	Green

- Bless and inscribe the candle with the person's name and "Develop musical ability."

- Light the candle, and place it on the altar in the center of your pentagram.

- Play some beautiful music while you are conducting this spell.

- Say your protection prayer for Friday, and recite the following:

Oh Angel of Venus, I desire to shine

Rhythm with harmony is to be mine.

[Say this spell six times, then say:]

So mote it be.

[Allow the candle to burn down and out.]

 A SPELL TO IMPROVE WRITING SKILLS

You need only perform this spell for three days.

Day: Begin on a Wednesday
Moon phase: Waxing
Candle color: Green or yellow

- Bless and inscribe the candle with the person's name and "To improve writing ability."

- Place the candle on the altar in the center of your pentagram.

- Light the candle.

- Place a book of literature on the altar.

- Say your protection prayer for Wednesday.

- Recite the following:

I summon the ruler of Mercury,

Archangel Raphael, guardian of the east,

To shower magic into my mind

So that my hands may write with vigor.

May I be filled with inspiration.

[Recite this six times, then say:]

And So mote it be.

[Then allow the candle to burn down and out.]

 A SPELL TO ENHANCE YOUR PSYCHIC ABILITY

This spell is essential to those of you who wish to take up spell-casting seriously. You should practice this spell every day for a week. Being well on the way to becoming a practicing witch, you must work to develop your psychic gifts. Perform this spell frequently for speedy results.

You will soon find yourself picking up small things on a psychic level—such as knowing who's on the other end of the phone before you answer it or dreaming about something that comes true. Your ability will develop steadily as you go along. It will help if you also focus on communicating with your guide and visualize yourself doing so, then put this idea into an imaginary ball and throw it out into the universe, because that should intensify the spell.

Day: Any day of the week
Moon phase: Any
Candle color: White or purple

- Bless and inscribe the candle with your name and "To become psychic."

- Anoint the candle, and place in the center of your pentagram.

- Light the candle.

- It is best to be very quiet when you are performing this spell.

- Say your protection prayer for whichever day it is.

- Perform your visualization with the glass ball while you sit before your altar.

- Recite the following once:

Angels of the cosmos, cast thy light toward me.
Give me psychic perception and insight so that I may
Communicate with life's forces.

I require the clairvoyance so that I may grow

And predict the future for all.

The spell is cast,

And So mote it be.

Meditate upon the candle for a few minutes before letting it burn down and out.

 A SPELL FOR WORLD PEACE

This spell should be conducted for nine nights.

Day:	Monday or Wednesday
Moon phase:	Waning
Candle color:	Purple or lilac

• Bless and anoint your candle, and inscribe the words, "World Peace" on it.

• Light the candle, and place in the center of your pentagram.

• Recite the following:

I summon all the angels of the universe

To look upon the earth and see the destruction that flows upon it.

Bring understanding to all those who plan to destroy.

Let them see that we have this precious creation you have given us.

Let no man starve, let no man destroy.

Let peace reign forevermore.

[Recite this nine times, then say:]

So mote it be.

[Then let the candle burn down and out.]

 A SPELL TO HELP WITH A LEGAL MATTER

This is a nine-day ritual.

Day:	Begin on a Thursday
Moon phase:	Waxing
Candle color:	Purple or lavender

- Bless and inscribe the candle with as much detail about the legal matter as you can.

- Inscribe the way you would like the situation to be.

- Anoint the candle, and place it in the center of your pentagram.

- Light the candle, and recite the following:

I summon and conjure the Archangel Sachiel, ruler of Jupiter,

To aid this magical practice.

I desire for the legal matter [say in detail what it is that you require]

To be brought forward in my favor.

Deliver all the power you possess, making me be successful at this time.

[Recite the spell seven times, then say:]

And So mote it be.

[Then let the candle burn down and out.]

Conclusion

THERE ARE SO MANY DIFFERENT FORMS OF MAGIC; the contents of this book just scratch the surface. It shows you the first steps to developing your potential and achieving your goals. Before you begin to really understand the "wise arts," you must follow the gentle rules so that you don't slip up and cast a spell for something you don't necessarily want.

I can't stress enough that once you have turned the key and unlocked the force that every one of us possesses, you must always conduct your rituals for the good and benefit of others or yourself. *Under no circumstances ever use magic for revenge or wrongdoing.*

Some of those whom you respect and feel close to may disapprove of your newfound interest, so be prepared to explain that witchcraft isn't a swearword. Remember that it is only their lack of knowledge that places fear in their souls. Many ancient scriptures have predicted that Paganism is on the increase and that in a few hundred years, many will revert back to the old religion. This seems to be the case, as more and more people are beginning to accept it.

While writing this book, I had no alternative but to tell certain members of my family that I was a witch and that I have been one for many years. Their first reaction was shock and even horror at the idea, but once they had read the book, they understood why I had always been a little different. Now I can happily display my pentagram and spellcast away to my heart's content.

Once you have searched your soul to find within yourself those things that feel right, you will achieve a sense of self-acceptance. After reading this, you may think that magic and spells are not for you and that you feel more comfortable sticking with your own beliefs. That's fine as well, because you will have broadened your knowledge, and you will have the facts of the matter, rather than silly or false ideas based on ignorance.

Many who have undertaken the wisdom of Wicca find that it changes their lives forever. They look at everything in more detail and strive to perfect their souls and personalities with each passing day. Some go on to read more about it, becoming experts themselves. Wicca is not rigid, so you won't be pushed or ushered in a particular way, and you won't be forced to give up any other beliefs that you may already have. You will find your true path in your own way, putting you into control of your destiny.

Good luck, and may the angels bless you all.

Acknowledgments

Special thanks Annette Gauden, who inspired me to write this book; my mother, who bought me dozens of books on the subject; and my guardian angel, who has helped me through some rough times and inspired me to find the good spells when I needed them.

Hampton Roads Publishing Company

...*for the evolving human spirit*

Hampton Roads Publishing Company publishes books on
a variety of subjects, including spirituality, health,
and other related topics.

For a copy of our latest catalog, call (978) 465-0504 or visit our
distributor's website at *www.redwheelweiser.com.* You can also sign
up for our newsletter and special offers by going to
www.redwheelweiser.com/newsletter